Mirror by Design

Mirror by Design

• Using Reflection to Transform Space •

Pamela Heyne

John Wiley & Sons, Inc.
New York • Chichester • Brisbane • Toronto • Singapore

This text is printed on acid-free paper.

Library of Congress Cataloging-in-Publication Data:

Heyne, Pamela.
Mirror by design : using reflection to transform space / Pamela Heyne.
p. cm.
Includes bibliographical references.
ISBN 0-471-11833-8 (cloth : alk. paper)
1. Mirrors in architecture. 2. Space (Architecture) I. Title.
NA2796.H485 1996
729--dc20 95-51484

Printed in the United States of America

10 9 8 7 6 5 4 3 2 1

To Carl, my loving and supportive husband.

Contents

Preface

Whenever I tell people that I am an architect with an interest in mirrors, I get the comment, "Oh, mirrors make spaces seem so much bigger." I then say, "Yes, but they do so much more..." This book attempts to complete that statement and to give you techniques to exploit the mirror's potential.

Yes, mirrors enhance space. And, less well known, they can bring us improved views from around the corner or from another level as with periscopes. Additionally, mirrors can flatter us and add sparkle, kaleidoscopic gaiety, and brilliant sun to the environment. They can also be so illusionary that we do not even know they exist.

This book's organization parallels the history of the mirror, which moved from small grooming aid to decorative accessory to larger scale architectural uses, as in Versailles or a modern Manhattan penthouse apartment. It will look at the Chinese art of placement, feng shui, and decorative approaches in Iran and India. The final chapter looks at dynamic effects, some of my favorite uses of the mirror. It will show a kaleidoscope skylight, view shifting, periscoping, heliostats bringing sunlight into interiors.

By employing the "law of reflection" the designer will know just which wall would be most effectively mirrored in an apartment, how to capture a beautiful view, or simply how high to place the bathroom light.

I am struck at how fast, inexpensive and neat much mirror work is. I jokingly call it "remodeling without plaster dust." In this era of shrinking spaces and shrinking budgets, the mirror can be a useful ally.

A fascinating implication of using mirrors, particularly to enhance space, is that the floor plan becomes less important. Even a "rabbit warren," hated by all architects, might be acceptable with some skillfully deployed mirrors. Chinese practitioners of feng shui have for centuries let the mirror make up for certain imperfect plans.

The mirror can improve upon the less than perfect, and it can make the splendid even more wonderful. Nirvana Penthouse is a tiny mirrored Manhattan restaurant, high above Central Park. It has a red tented ceiling that contrasts with the cool reflections of distant skyscrapers and stars at night. Everyone in the restaurant has a wonderful view, whether real or illusionary. Similarly, a basement periscope window I created for clients gives a beautiful view of sky, trees, and lawn. It is not real of course; it is simply an illusion, but so much more appealing than looking at a blank wall.

The mirror is a delightful, affordable tool. Kings paid ransoms and fomented intrigues to learn the secrets for making it. Now it is yours to use, by design.

Many deserve thanks and appreciation. Nancy Duncan helped mightily with calls and checking. Dr. Christine Kleinegger, curator of the exhibit "Mirrors: Reflections of Society and Self" at the New York State Museum in Albany provided new insights. Russ Barker, Jim Mack, and the staff and members of the North American Association of Mirror Manufacturers were most helpful, as were Caroline Backlund at the National Gallery of Art Library, Jean Miller at the Folger Library, and Virginia Wright and Jill Thomas-Clark at the Corning Museum of Glass. Thanks also to Bob Thompson, Matt Forrest, and to Chris Ashworth and his staff and associates. Lastly, Amanda Miller, Ira Brodsky, and all at Wiley deserve a final bow.

Mirror by Design

1

The Glorious Chameleon

"*The mirror is seen in nature* in the surfaces of lakes, in the hollows of the mountains and in the pools deep in the shadow of the trees; in winding ribbons of the rivers that catch and give back the flying birds, clouds and blue sky. A dreary thing to have that element leave the landscape. It may be as refreshing and beautifying in architecture, if architecturally used." (Frank Lloyd Wright, *Architectural Record,* 1928)

The mirror is one of the most fascinating of all design materials because of its changeableness. Often called the chameleon of architecture, it can look completely different in use because of the reflections that play on its surface. It is also incredibly versatile, helping us in our daily grooming routines, enhancing spatial perceptions, shifting and focusing views and light, and dematerializing mass.

The essence of the mirror is most often silver, the brightest substance in nature. The silver is sprayed onto clear glass, the function of which is to stabilize the silver. A metal amalgam is applied to promote adherence; the mirror is then coated with copper and paint to prevent scratching and corrosion. Variations on this theme are numerous. Today we have available to us transparent or "one-way" mirrors; first-surface mirrors; beveled, patterned, tinted, coated, and antiqued mirrors; mirrored tiles; various types of safety mirrors; and plastic mirrors.

Although the mirror was readily available to Frank Lloyd Wright, and although he was cognizant of the mirror's potential, he rarely used it. He, like many designers in his generation, experimented with open plans and dematerialization of outer walls with glass, not mirrors. But, in recent years, designers have seen that the mirror can substitute illusionary space for real space or make outer walls less oppressive, all without installing steel beams. Our homes and apartments are often smaller than we might wish, the open plan has been under attack for various reasons, construction budgets are often more stringent than in the past. Many buildings and additions to buildings are now constructed underground, with no possibility of natural views. Mirrors are important in these settings for creating a sense of spaciousness, for bringing in additional sunlight, and, from time to time, for creating artificial views. Even views above ground are less pristine than in the past. Indeed, Wright's studio, Taliesin West, though beautiful and remote, is approached via a subdivision and looks out onto a desert and other subdivisions.

Space: When considering the mirror, people often say, "It makes spaces so much bigger." Actually, it makes spaces "seem" so much bigger. But for many, the illusion becomes a psychological reality. This can apply to the garden, as well as to the interior (see Plate 1). The mirrors that we have seen on commercial buildings can easily be adapted to the smaller scale garden. Today, as smaller homes are becoming a reality for many of us and as the open plan is rethought, traditional framed mirrors, paneled mirrors (see Figure 1.1), and wall and ceiling mirrors can all add new dimensions. Multiple reflections and infinity chambers might give a more dazzling festive sense of space. Wright said of these effects, "But now the walls might disappear, the ceilings too, and—yes—the floors as well. Why not? In certain cases. Nicely calculated effects of this sort might amplify and transform a cabinet into a realm, a room into bewildering vistas and avenues, a single unit into unlimited areas of color, pattern and form" (*Architectural Record,* 1928).

Views: Spatial expansion is but one aspect of the designer's mirror. The mirror is extremely important in shifting views (see Plate 2). Do we have an unattractive view of our neighbor's brick wall outside our dining room window? No matter: Mirroring a window jamb or installing an angled mirror bay window can give us a better view. Is our office in a dark, depressing basement? A periscope window can bring in a view of gardens and sunlight. In the 18th century, the English poet Samuel Rogers had his window shutters covered with mirrors to enhance his fine view of the Thames River. The English landscape architect Humphrey Repton installed mirrors in gardens to convey improved views. Benjamin Franklin invented a view shifter to be mounted outside a second-story window in order to see who was knocking at the door. It was called the Philadelphia Busybody.

Figure 1.1 *Versailles, bedroom of Louis XIV, French, late 17th /early 18th century. The mirror's illusionary qualities were amplified by recessing it in paneling. Even in the smallest apartment, the idea is relevant today. © Photo RMN.*

Light: Mirrors have long been used to enhance light. In the 18th century, candle holders were often attached to mirror frames to increase light. Light emanating from mirrors can also be festive and unexpected. Dance floors and bars, in particular, have exploited this type of reflectivity. In more serene environments, modern kitchens and bathrooms are brightened—and save energy—with mirrors placed adjacent to the lighting fixtures. The mirrors literally double the amount of light when combined in this fashion. In recent years, architects have experimented with light scoops or heliostats, installing canted mirrors outside or near clerestory windows to bounce sunlight into lower reaches. Interestingly, studies have shown that sunlight is more important than views for the emotional well-being of workers in underground facilities (see Plate 3). Although this idea seems novel, similar concepts have existed in Paris for years. Mirrored flaps are sometimes installed outside windows to capture and send sunlight indoors, which is often precious, particularly in winter months. Although it seems straight out of science fiction, in 1994 the Russians orbited their Mir spacecraft to reflect sunlight into northern regions as an experiment in lengthening growing seasons.

The ray of sun that is shifted can easily be focused, creating a multiplication of the heat attached to that ray. This is an aspect of mirrors that has been exploited by ancient peoples, and has been a source of inspiration and experimentation for modern architects and designers.

Dematerializing mass: Mirrors applied in a space will make it seem larger. Mirrors applied on a solid object will make the object seem smaller. The French installed mirrors on piers between glass windows in order to make those piers seem less massive. Department store designers often do the same thing. We can similarly put mirror on a piece of furniture to make it less visible, enabling it to "disappear" in reflections. The mirrored cube for plants or sculpture also disappears in reflections (see Figure 1.2).

The person in the mirror: The mirror has been a necessary toilet article for more than 6000 years. We rarely leave our homes without looking at it. It has fascinating psychological associations. Used in public areas, a mirror can take the curse off a "bad" table at the back of the room as we see others reflected in it. It can make us feel more secure near cash machines and in elevators. Used in elevator lobbies, it can quiet complaints about slow elevators as we adjust our clothes. Those of us who are messy will be neater with mirrors. If we are romantically inclined, mirrors might make us more so. Honeymoon suites use lavish amounts of mirror.

We are so used to seeing our reflections reversed that we do not think there is any other way to observe our faces. But recently, an inventor, John Walter, began marketing the "true mirror" that uses combined mirrors to give us a true reflection. This is important for people wanting to gain better insights into their true selves, according to Mr. Walter.

Mirrors are important to help babies gain self-awareness, and to help with the development of motor skills. Fascinated by their reflections, babies will crawl toward mirrors or pull themselves up to see their faces. Plastic mirrors are an integral part of day care centers and preschool environments.

Mirrors can help some mentally ill persons gain a new sense of esteem or acceptance; for others, they may be a source of confusion. For some suffering from Alzheimer's disease, mirrors might convey the image of "a stranger" in their reflections. Sometimes we like seeing our reflections; sometimes we don't.

Figure 1.2 *Mirrored stands disappear in their own reflections. Courtesy of Bassett Mirror Co., Inc.*

The mirror as a design tool: The mirror's changeableness occasionally makes some people a bit nervous about using it. They worry that the mirror will look "cold." On the other hand, they worry that it might look "flashy." Additionally, they are nervous about knowing just what will be reflected by the mirror.

Another comment heard with some regularity is "Oh, what a beautiful mirror." What is usually meant in this comment is "Oh, what a beautiful mirror frame."

The mirror is not inherently cold or flashy, nor is the mirror inherently beautiful. The mirror is inherently neutral. We who design with it and use it can give it whatever character we wish. It will reflect what we want it to reflect and can assume diverse styles, from sleekly contemporary to elegant and traditional. With tints or a lattice cover, it can be subtle. In combinations, it can convey infinity and give us large-scale kaleidoscopic effects. As we learn more about the law of reflection, we can see how to reflect just what we want and how to "cover up" reflections we don't want. We learn how to control the changeableness of the chameleon of architecture.

Two distinct advantages of working with mirrors are time and cost. A mirror wall can be installed in about an hour. Its price has consistently gone down over the years and will be a fraction of the price of removing a structural wall. One could call it "remodeling without plaster dust."

Now You See It, Now You Don't

Hugh Jacobsen, the archjtect, gave a succinct definition of the mirror. He said, "A mirror is a mirror when you can see yourself; otherwise it is an illusionary means of expanding space." We have all had the experience of assuming we could walk into a certain "space," only to see our reflections at the last minute, realizing that we are simply seeing an illusion of space. Designers from the time of Versailles have realized the spatial impact of mirrors above eye level. The important Room of the Bull's-Eye at Versailles contains a false bull's-eye window—constructed of mirror—above the fireplace. The Kärntner Bar by Adolf Loos in Vienna has mirrors above eye level in the tiny space. The English designer, Sir John Soane, placed mirrors in small niches and upper reaches of some of his designs.

Modern developers trying to exploit a magnificent view may put a mirror in a far corner of the room adjacent to that view. The illusions will be compelling selling points for the developer. He or she will have emphasized the view and the space of the dwelling rather than the fact the buyer is looking at a mirror. Without realizing it, the developer may have been using mirrors the way the magician would, by emphasizing the oblique view.

The phrase "it's all done with mirrors" derives from magic tricks. Magicians know that a mirror viewed obliquely, particularly at a 45-degree angle, will cover up the lower limbs of an assistant, giving the illusion that the limbs have disappeared and become sheer space (see Figure 1.3). In actuality, the canted mirror merely reflects the curtains at the side of the stage, which look just like the curtains at the back of the space. This simple idea has been the basis for numerous disappearing acts over time. Magicians understand the optics of the mirror. We who wish to create magical effects with mirrors need to understand optics as well.

How does the mirror work? The mirror reflects light more perfectly than any other substance. Of course, unless it is exceptionally dark, we see all objects and people because of the light that they reflect. Generally, that light is reflected in a "diffuse" fashion (see Figure 1.4). For mirrors, however, the light is reflected in a predictable fashion according to the law of reflection. That law states, simply: The angle of incidence is equal and opposite to the angle of reflection (see Figure 1.5). For example, the light emanating from a house plant bounces off the mirror's surface and enters our eyes, causing us to see the plant "in" the mirror. We see a "virtual illusion." Unless writing is involved, the reversal of objects in the mirror usually is not bothersome to us.

An object that is reflected in the mirror will seem as far back from the surface of the mirror as it actually is in front of the mirror. For instance, if the house plant is placed two

Figure 1.3 *The mirror at a 45-degree angle has been the basis of many magic tricks. From Hopkins,* Magic, *1901. Courtesy of the Library of Congress, Rare Book Division.*

feet in front of the mirror, it will seem two feet back in the mirror's illusionary space. The reflection will seem a total of four feet away from the actual plant.

Similarly, if we ourselves stand two feet in front of the mirror, our reflections will seem to be four feet away. Although we are looking closely at our faces in the mirror as we comb our hair or shave, in reality we are looking at a face that is much smaller than what we think it is. People are amazed to learn that their reflected face is only half the size it is in reality. Drawing an outline on a steamy mirrored surface proves the point. If we were to take a picture of ourselves in the mirror, we would have to set the camera for the distance of our image rather than the surface of the mirror. In this example, it would have to be set for four feet.

If we look at the mirror quite closely and obliquely, we might notice two reflections: that created by the silver and that created by the glass, say ¼ inch in front of the silver. This is rarely a problem in interior design situations. For scientific instruments and specialized items such as cameras or small kaleidoscopes, however, the first-surface mirror is usually specified. It consists of a thin metallic coating on the front of the glass. Obviously, it is more fragile than a mirror with glass, silver, and its various protective coatings.

Figure 1.4 *Diffuse reflection, as from a plaster wall.*

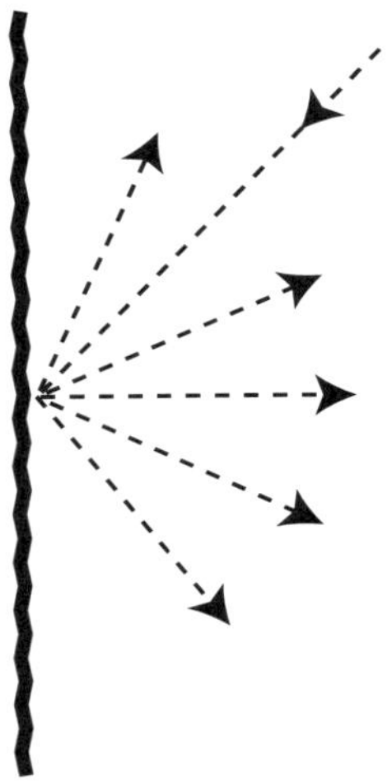

Figure 1.5 *Reflection from a plane mirror. Angle of incidence is equal and opposite to angle of reflection.*

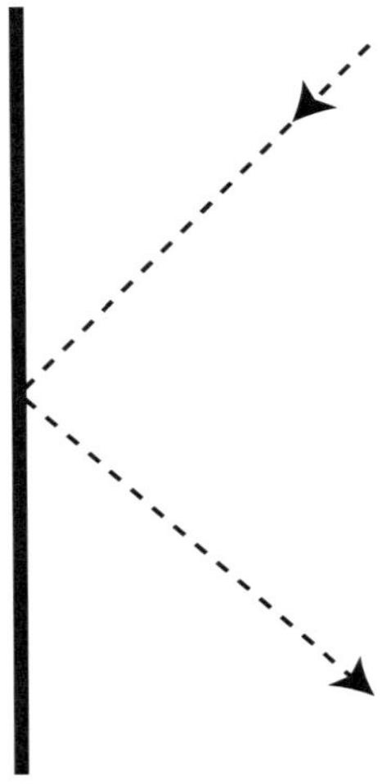

Figure 1.6 *Transparent mirror. Some light is reflected; the rest is absorbed and transmitted.*

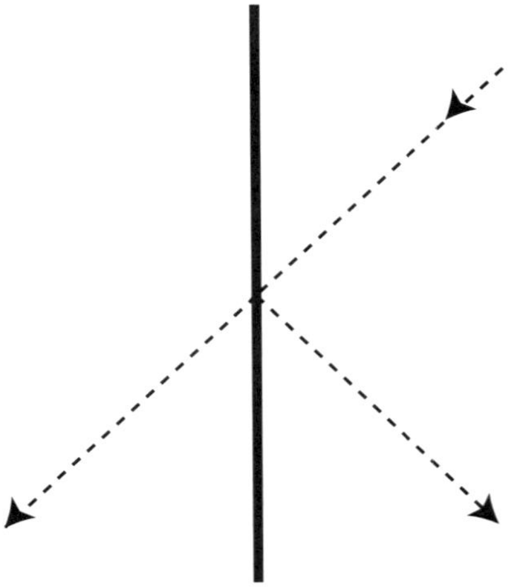

Transparent mirrors have been called one-way mirrors or mirror glass (see Figure 1.6). Variations of these mirrors have appeared in settings as diverse as magic shows (see Figures 1.7a and 1.7b), casinos, police station line-ups, psychiatric wards, and modern office buildings. Sometimes they consist of one layer of glass, sometimes two layers in order to protect the reflective coating. One-way mirrors will seem less bright than ordinary mirrors since, of course, less than 100 percent of the light striking them is reflected. Similarly, tinted and antiqued mirrors are less bright than regular mirrors, since they absorb some of the light that strikes them.

Figure 1.7a *At the turn of the century, transparent mirror was a popular magic trick. From Hopkins,* Magic, *1901. Courtesy of the Library of Congress, Rare Book Division.*

Figure 1.7b *Since some light is transmitted, depending on lighting conditions, one can see through this mirror.*

The mirror at a 45-degree angle is the basis of seeing around a corner and the basis of magic tricks. At this angle, we do not see our own reflection, but, rather, the reflection from the side (see Figure 1.8).

A mirror that is viewed obliquely is, in essence, using the 45-degree angle. An example of this use of a mirror is a simple plan of a townhouse. The townhouse is a natural candidate for mirror because of the minimal number of windows. But, where should the mirror be placed? While many locations are possible, one intriguing possibility is to place the mirror on the diagonal from the entrance which, in this case, permits a person entering the house to gain a view of the rear garden in the mirror long before seeing the garden

Figure 1.9 *Mirror viewed obliquely. A mirrored wall on the diagonal will reflect a view of the rear yard to people entering the house.*

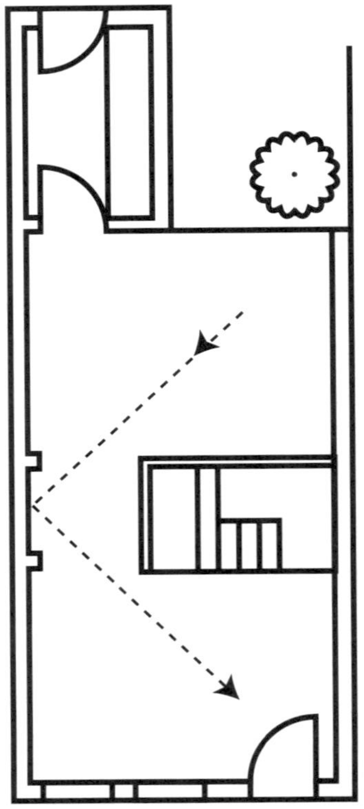

Figure 1.8 *Mirror at a 45-degree angle, the basis of magic tricks and seeing around a corner.*

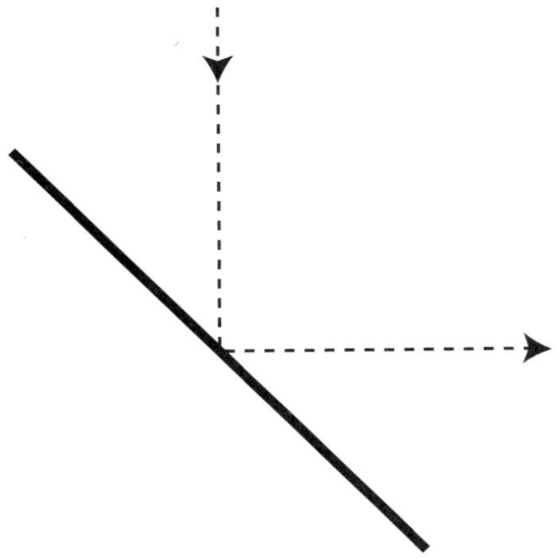

in reality. Since the person entering the house initially does not see his or her reflection, this can be surprising and illusionary. The author executed a similar installation for Jim van Sweden, the landscape architect. Guests, new to the home, often asked if Jim had purchased the house next door. They thought that they were looking into an illusionary space rather than simply a mirrored wall (see Figure 1.9).

The mirror at 45 degrees can be combined with another parallel mirror to create a periscope. Since the ray of light is reflected twice, it is not reversed. Periscopes convey the images of ships going in the correct direction, for instance (see Figure 1.10). If two canted mirrors are not parallel but at right angles, however, a reverse periscope is the result (see Figure 1.11).

Convex mirrors make objects seem smaller. This is the basis of the 19th-century girandole (see Figure 1.12). At the far end of a room, it gave a miniaturized, compressed view of an entire room. This was also the basis of many ancient mirrors. Convex mirrors permitted a small, hand-held mirror to reflect the whole person. This is the basis of our

Figure 1.10 *Periscope. Light bounces from one mirror to the other.*

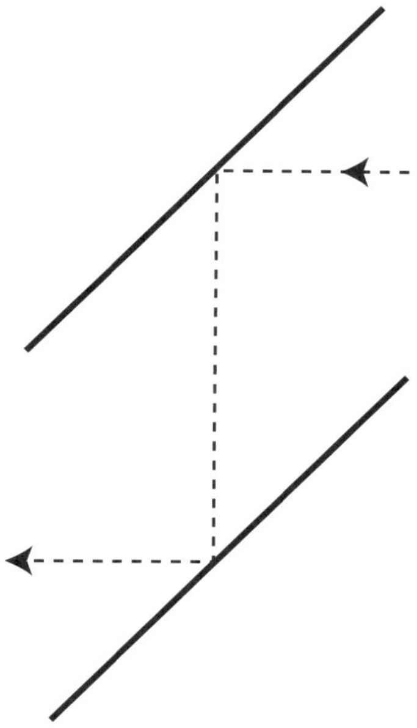

Figure 1.11 *Reverse periscope.*

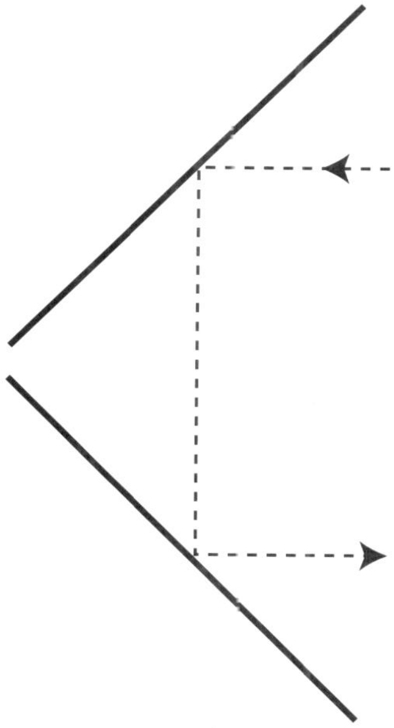

automobile rear-view and side-view mirrors as well. An amusing scene occurred in the movie *Jurassic Park*. As a dinosaur was closing in on a speeding car, it was first visible in the side-view mirror with the inscription underneath, "Objects are larger than they appear."

Concave mirrors tend to make reflected objects look larger in size (see Figure 1.13). This is the basis of many of our modern bathroom grooming mirrors. Concave mirrors were also used by early humans to create fires, and were called "burning mirrors." The ancient Greeks determined that parabolic, rather than spherical, mirrors were better at creating fires, since the light was reflected to one point. The ancient Romans used concave mirrors in amorous settings as a means of heightening sensory pleasure.

Concave mirrors also have the dazzling ability to create "real," as opposed to "virtual," illusions. With proper tolerances, design, and lighting, an object placed on a concave mirror can seem to "float" in front of the viewer. This is the basis of an amusing parlor trick manufactured by Opti-Gone Associates and marketed as the Mirage. A container holding a piece of chocolate will be offered to the guest, who will find it is simply an illusion, floating in air. It is not a hologram; it is a real illusion (see Figure 1.14). A custom model was installed at Disneyworld under a table. It creates the illusion of chocolate chip cookies sitting on a plate. Of course, these cookies can only be seen—not touched, and certainly not eaten.

Other materials are "mirrorlike" because they create reflections. We humans have long placed particular value on shimmering items. Our television advertisements today point to this fascination: the glistening wood tabletop, the dish that comes from the dish-

Figure 1.12 *Convex mirror.*

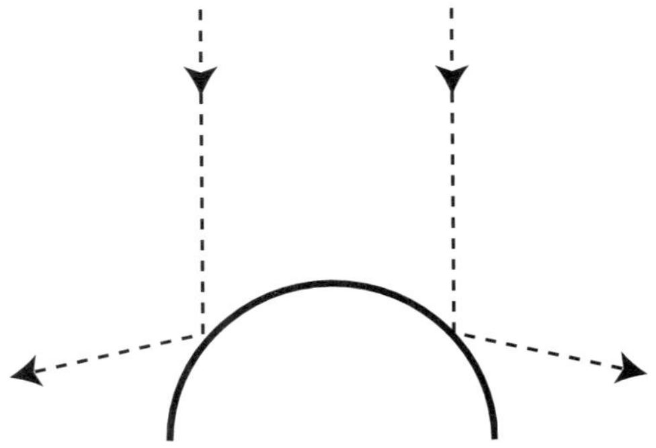

Figure 1.13 *Concave mirror.*

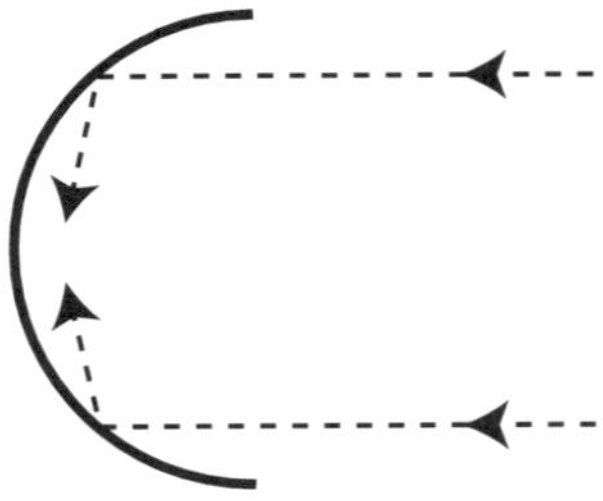

washer so immaculate that the mother-in-law can see her face in it, the hair that gleams like gold. Indeed, the world's currencies are based on stockpiles of gleaming gold and silver.

Since reflections can be created on many different materials, numerous substances have performed the role of mirrors in the past. Polished stones, finely crafted metals, even bowls of water all cast reflections. The earliest mirrors made by humans were hand mirrors. They have been intimately linked with everyday life since prehistoric times, and have been particularly important to women. Studies of primitive cultures show, not surprisingly, that women have used physical beauty to attract wealthy men, whose market value is dependent more on power and wealth than on physical appearance. So closely allied are mirrors with women that the biological symbol of the female is a hand mirror (see Figure 1.15).

Figure 1.14 *The Mirage. Objects placed inside the device appear to rest on top of the two-inch circle. This three-dimensional effect is created with mirrors. Courtesy of Opti-Gone Associates.*

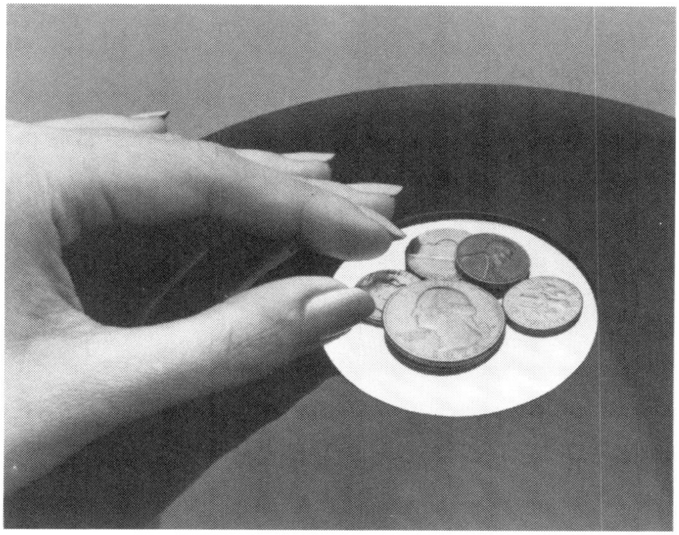

Figure 1.15 *The female biological symbol is based on the hand-held mirror.*

Superstitions and Traditions

Most of us have, since childhood, said "seven years' bad luck" when we break a mirror. The phrase, "seven years' bad luck" actually originated in a fortune-telling ceremony in Greece and Rome. In the sixth century B.C., the Greeks developed a practice of divination called catoptromancy, or scrying. Earthenware or glass bowls would be filled with water and a person's reflections in the water—moratorium to the Romans—would be read by a mirror seer. If the mirror slipped and broke, that was an indication of bad luck. In the Roman era, a belief developed that a person's health changed in cycles of 7 years. Hence, a broken mirror meant seven years of bad luck (Panati, p. 11).

Other superstitions remain in our modern culture. The concept of the soul's presence in the mirror is a powerful one, often associated with death. Certain Mediterranean cultures still place a cloth over a mirror in the room of a dying person so that the soul will not take flight from the mirror, but will be borne away by the ghost of the deceased. In films, the vampire, who has surmounted death, possesses no reflection. In the opera *The Tales of Hoffman*, Hoffman is lured into a romantic entanglement with Giulietta and loses his reflection in the process.

Some long-standing superstitions are delightful vestiges of a more primitive past. Iranians, for instance, celebrate the arrival of spring with a colorful celebration called Nowruz. They set a colorful table with symbolic dishes relating to happiness, prosperity, and rebirth. A mirror is placed on the table to reflect creation and give the participants a sense of their heritage.

Development of the Mirror

Although mirrors have been with us for more than 6000 years, the glass mirror, appropriate as an interior decorative device, is just over 300 years old. The evolution of the mirror from a small toilet article to the smooth, clear, reflective surface we see today is a tale of fascinating discoveries, artistry, and, by the 17th century, intense foreign intrigue.

The first mirror in nature was undoubtedly a still pond of water. One can imagine how surprising reflections must have been in prehistoric times. We get a sense of the wonderment and attempt to understand natural phenomena in early myths. In the Greek myth of Narcissus, a youth fell in love with another beautiful youth whom he saw in a still pool of water. At first he did not realize that it was his own reflection, and spurned the love of Echo and all others. Punished by the gods for his arrogance, he was transformed into the flower that bears his name, and Echo was changed into the stone that mysteriously "speaks." Even after Aristotle studied light reflections and said they were similar to sound reflections, the charm of the early story remains.

For thousands of years, in spite of their everyday usefulness as toilet articles, mirrors were also considered to have mystical properties. They might be attributes of gods or priests. In various cultures, mirrors were used to produce smoke and fires, create illusions, help foretell the future, or detect crimes and infidelities. They often symbolized the soul. Their prevalence in ancient graves attests to their symbolic importance.

The first man-made mirrors were fashioned from stones. An early slate mirror and a selenite mirror with traces of a wooden frame were found in the region of El-Badari, a civilization of pre-dynastic Egypt, dating from 4500 B.C. When moistened, the slate became an effective mirror.

North American Indians also created mirrors out of slate and mica. Particularly interesting stone mirrors were the Aztecs' obsidian mirrors, made from a naturally fused black glass emanating from the eruptions of volcanoes. The obsidian would flake easily and could attain a high degree of polish. The mirrors had personal and religious importance. Mirrors adorned the eyes of statues of the Aztecs' most important gods, one of whom was the god of war, the "god of the terrible eyes." When the Aztecs first saw Spaniards, some of whom were wearing eyeglasses, they said the Spaniards had the eyes of their war god. The early Olmecs used iron oxides, such as hematite and pyrite (fool's gold), for their mirrors; the Incas had particularly sophisticated mirrors of silver, gold, and bronze, and used concave mirrors to create fire. Although most early artifacts, including mirrors, were destroyed or melted down by the Spaniards, some of those early mirrors were brought to Europe as spoils. Diego de Soto described "a mirror with two faces; a mirror with the head of a lion; a mirror with the figure of an owl" (Goldberg, p. 92).

The first metal mirrors appeared at approximately 3000 B.C. in the Indus Valley and in Egypt. Mirrors were particularly important throughout the entire Egyptian culture (see Figure 1.16) . Worked of copper, bronze, silver, and gold, they were highly polished, slightly convex, and shaped like the solar disk, a slightly flattened circle representing the sun at sunset or sunrise. "The Egyptians regarded the polished disks of their mirrors as a symbol of the sun, for the mirrors were able to pick up its rays and give off light as did the great life-giver of the universe...their sun-god, Ra" (Goldberg, p. 27). High priests also understood rudimentary mirror optics, creating magic illusions and reflecting sunlight into tombs and pyramids under construction. They used mirrors during ceremonial occasions and entombed them with mummies. During festive occasions, dancers performed holding mirrors.

Figure 1.16 *Egyptian mirror on stand, c. 1479–1425 B.C. Reflector is silver and wood handle (partly restored) is sheathed in gold. Courtesy of the Metropolitan Museum of Art, Fletcher Fund, 1920.*

Egyptian wall paintings show women looking at their reflections in small mirrors, a necessity since they (and men) wore cosmetics. Some mirrors were small and portable, stored in the equivalent of a modern handbag. Some mirrors had elaborate handles, charmingly embellished with representations of gods, goddesses, or nude serving maids.

Mirrors are mentioned in the Bible. In a portion of Exodus, Moses is described as constructing the religious tabernacle with the aid of and sacrifice of his people: "And he made the laver of brass, and the foot of it of brass, of the mirrors of the women assembling, which assembled at the door of the tabernacle of the congregation" (Exodus 38:8).

Although Egyptians occasionally produced small glass mirrors, metal mirrors remained the norm in Egypt and in subsequent Greek and Roman cultures, in the Orient, and in Europe. Sixth- and fifth-century B.C. Greek mirrors contained magnificently decorated handles embellished with images of humans, animals, and mythological creatures. The mirrors were often able to stand on a table, although some have been shown affixed to a wall by a nail. The Greeks also made important contributions to the studies of optics. Aristotle, Heron, and Diocles analyzed various aspects of reflection.

Mirrors were both popular and plentiful in Rome. Even serving maids had mirrors. Mirrors were also incorporated into some wall decorations. By A.D. 40, full-length mirrors, crafted of gold and silver and encrusted with jewels, adorned the rooms of the wealthy. Concave mirrors enhanced some sexual fantasies. Seneca discussed a rich man named Hostius Quadra: "Mirrors faced him on all sides in order that he might be a spectator of his own shame" (Goldberg, p. 113). For Seneca, however, mirrors had a higher purpose. They were intended for self-knowledge, not for indulgence.

Although most mirrors of this period were metal, the Romans did produce small glass mirrors, learning the technique from their Egyptian subjects. Metal mirrors, however, would remain the dominant form, throughout the Roman Empire, northern Europe, and the Orient. Delicately incised fifth-century B.C. bronze and gold Celtic mirrors, found in graves, attest to their sophisticated artistry, and to the value the owners placed on mirrors. Bronze and gold mirrors originating in China were also elaborately decorated on their backs, with styles and content varying with the dynasties. A favorite image in the T'ang Dynasty, for example, was a magpie, which would indicate marital infidelity. The concept of feng shui originated in China in the ninth century B.C. to become an all-encompassing philosophy designed to create harmonious surroundings. Mirrors helped to deflect both negative and positive forces, and to bring light to difficult corners.

Japanese mirrors were influenced by the Chinese, but with simpler ornamentation on the back. A curiosity in Chinese and Japanese mirrors is the so-called magic mirror. Sunlight striking the front of a convex mirror would project an image on a nearby wall.

That image curiously contained the characters from the back. The explanation was fairly simple. The pattern of the characters from the rear, though imperceptible from the front, was still engraved just behind the convex surface and would be projected when lit by an intense beam of sunlight when struck from the front (Goldberg, p. 55).

Glass

The history of mirrors is intimately linked to the history of glass, for while mirrors remained predominantly metal, they would rarely attain great size due to their weight and cost. And although glass consists of some of the most plentiful items in the earth—sand, soda, and limestone—centuries would elapse before glass would become the transparent, smooth, and expansive substance we take for granted today. Sand, or silica, requires extremely high temperatures to fuse. The addition of soda permits fusion at lower temperatures. This is known as a flux. When these two ingredients are heated, the soda melts and the sand dissolves in the molten soda. When cooled, this product, called "water glass," is not impervious to water. However, the addition of lime renders the glass waterproof. Today, an average batch mix for flat glass is about 70 percent silica sand, 12 percent soda, 13 percent lime, and small amounts of other substances. The final composition is a soda-lime-silicate virtually unaffected by moisture or acids.

The origin of glass is in the Middle East, probably in Syria about 2500 B.C. The Roman historian Pliny gave his account of the discovery of glass in 77 A.D. in his *Naturalis Historica*. Writing of a beach in Phoenicia with glistening white sands, he said, "There is a story that once a ship belonging to some traders in natural soda (natron, an Egyptian product) put in here and that they scattered along the shore to prepare a meal. Since, however, no stones suitable for supporting their cauldrons were forthcoming, they rested them on lumps of soda from their cargo. When these became heated and were completely mingled with the sand on the beach a strange translucent liquid flowed forth in streams; and this, it is said, was the origin of glass." The reason that the sailors traveled with blocks of soda on board was its importance in trade. It was used in mummification procedures in Egypt and elsewhere around the Mediterranean. While there is debate about whether Pliny's account is true or not, ancient Egyptian texts do document early importation of glass from the area around the Phoenician beach which had particularly white, sparkling sands.

Glass has often been compared to ice because of its aesthetic characteristics. However, it differs from ice in its chemical structure. When water is cooled to form ice, it develops an ordered crystal structure. Sand, in its natural state, has a crystalline structure. When it is melted, however, the structure of the atoms becomes random. When it is cooled, the structure remains random, permitting transparency.

The first examples of glass we have are in the form of ornamental glass beads and rods. Glass beads have been uncovered in Egypt dating from 2500 B.C., and glass rods from Babylon have been found from an even earlier period. Skillfully colored glass beads, occasionally in the forms of animals, were important for adornment and trading throughout the Middle East, northern Europe, and China. Even when Columbus arrived in America, he noted in his diary that he traded red caps and glass beads with the native people.

For more than 2000 years, glassmaking was a slow, labor-intensive process. A small Egyptian bottle would be made by dipping a metal rod containing a blob of clay and dung at the end into molten glass. The rod was rotated to create a smoothly contoured shape. Elaboration, consisting of contrasting bands of color, handles, and bases, was also added. After the glass cooled, the core was picked out by hand using a sharp object. Many of these elegantly worked bottles have been found.

Eventually, the core dipping method was replaced by a revolutionary technique, glassblowing. By blowing through a metal rod and rotating a blob of molten glass, a hollow vessel could be produced more quickly. Discovered in about 50 B.C. on the Syria-Palestine coast, the technique quickly spread to Rome, and glass cups replaced metal cups as a status symbol among the wealthy. Additionally, for the first time, ordinary citizens could afford glass objects for everyday life. Not until the 19th and 20th centuries would glass objects be as prevalent for ordinary people. In addition to being found in homes, businesses, restaurants, and the Roman equivalent of bars, glass products were used as containers for shipments of oils, condiments, and foodstuffs, since they would not impart taste and could be reused.

The Romans exhibited great skill with their glass products. They eventually combined blowing with molding, having illustrations of gladiators or inscriptions of toasts such as "to your health" on the outside of glassware. Luxurious pieces of colored glass canes were combined to form bowls. Three-dimensional carving was perfected, along with cameo carving, painted surfaces, wheel-abraded surfaces, and enameling. Small, flat glass mirrors, about the size of modern compact mirrors, have been found with plaster frames. Later, blown glass bubbles were coated with lead on the concave side, with the mirrors intended to be seen from the convex side. A small convex mirror at the Corning Museum of Glass produces a startlingly good, albeit convex and dark, reflection (see Figure 1.17).

Figure 1.17 *A highly polished early glass convex mirror mounted in a bone frame, 4th–5th century A.D., late Roman Empire, probably from Egypt with Jewish religious significance. Courtesy of the Corning Museum of Glass.*

Even though the Romans were skilled at glass manufacture, and did produce window glass, they did not develop the large sheets of clear flat glass that are appropriate for decorative mirrors. The Romans were able to cast flat glass; a 32-inch-by-44-inch piece has been found at Pompeii. They also created crown glass, produced by spinning molten glass to form a large, round, flat piece. In addition, they were able to produce glass using the cylinder or muff process—an elongated bubble of glass that was slit and flattened (Engle, p. 79). Pliny wrote of having glass doors, "specularia." However, wood shutters and alabaster were more commonly used.

As the Roman Empire extended on all borders of the Mediterranean and northward through Italy, France, England, and parts of Germany, so too did the glass manufacturing houses. Roman glass technology spread throughout Europe, retaining a tentative foothold even after the fall of Rome and invasions of northern tribes. The medieval glass manufacturing houses were often continuations of Roman glass houses. In 678 Wilfrid, the Bishop of York, raved about the improvement installing glass windows made in the restoration of a church: "Light shone within, yet birds and rain could not penetrate" (Jope, p. 53).

The Byzantine Empire kept the art of glassmaking alive after the fall of the Roman Empire. The Byzantines created new forms and new decorative techniques. Lamps and tall-necked ceremonial flasks to prevent rapid evaporation were hallmarks of their work. The glass was enameled, incised, and often contained transparent colors. Lamps from Byzantium were often highly prized ornaments in Gothic churches. Some of the elaborate ornamentation has aesthetic motifs deriving from China. At this time, Chinese glass was made to resemble jade rings and carvings.

Glassmaking gained new importance in Europe with the development of the soaring Gothic cathedrals. "'A blaze of Glass windows' was a 12th-century chronicler's description of Canterbury Cathedral following its rebuilding in the new style. A few conservative churchmen even found the new brilliance too glaring, but the public enthusiastically applauded the stained glass, manufactured in the forest, where fuel and raw materials were available and where the smoke provoked no protest" (Gies, p. 132). Ashes from hardwood trees, preferably beech, provided the necessary soda for the manufacture of the glass. Colors were initially obtained by varying the melting time; eventually, metallic oxides were added. Copper resulted in red, iron in yellow, and manganese in purple (Gies, p. 133). Brilliantly colored glass windows were didactic, designed to convey religious instruction to the largely illiterate population. Clear glass was still difficult to produce, so most mirrors in the Middle Ages were still made of metal, called speculum. Mirrors were made of highly polished metal, and were often attached to a cord that could dangle from a woman's waist.

By the 13th century Venice was an important producer of sophisticated glass products. The Venetians had produced glass since 600 A.D. and had imported glass lamps and vessels from Byzantium. Additionally, they had access to the glistening sand needed from Syria. In 1279, Venetian glassmakers formed a guild. In 1292, Venetian city officials forced glassmakers to set up their shops on the island of Murano, fearing the possibility of fire from the intense heat of the ovens. The removal to Murano also served to keep the glassmaking processes secret.

Murano was about an hour away from Venice by boat, and it was a vacation center for the wealthy. Glassmakers often attained great social standing, and their daughters were able to marry into the aristocracy. However, there was a dark side to their success. Workers were forbidden to emigrate under threat of death.

Venetians began producing the first smooth glass mirrors at the beginning of the 14th century. They found a way to press a metallic leaf to the glass, and exported their mirrors throughout Europe (Goldberg, p. 138). At this time, the Netherlands and Germany also produced mirrors. In 1373, Nuremburg had a guild for glass mirrors, producing the convex mirrors of the same name. In the Nuremburg process, molten tin was introduced into the glass bubble while it was still hot. Germany made mirrors for the wealthy as well as individuals on holy pilgrimages. Worshipers would use mirrors to capture reflections of the religious scene.

Venice quickly overtook its northern European rivals, however. Two significant developments boosted Venice's superiority in mirrormaking. In 1460 a glassmaker, Angelo Beroviero, invented a new, clearer glass, called *cristallo* because of its thinness and clarity. Half a century later, in 1507, Andrea and Domenico d'Anzolo del Gallo developed the tin amalgam process, which became known as mirror foiling. Unlike earlier glass mirror-making processes, in the tin amalgam process, the metal did not have to be applied to small sheets or spheres of glass while it was hot. Now, larger, brighter mirrors could be produced more easily. The del Gallos submitted a petition to the Venetian authorities, claiming that they possessed "the secret of making good and perfect mirrors of crystalline glass, a precious and singular thing unknown to the whole world." They requested the exclusive privilege of manufacturing mirrors for 25 years.

During this time, the cylinder or muff process was used for the glass. The molten glass was blown into an elongated bubble. The ends were removed, and the bubble was slit and flattened (see Figures 1.18 and 1.19). After annealing and cooling, the glass was polished. Then, tin, hammered into thin sheets, was spread out smoothly and coated with mercury. Next, the tin was covered with paper. In the final step, the glass was laid down on the

Figure 1.18 *Detail of cylinder method of making glass, from* Encyclopedie *by Denis Diderot, 18th century. Courtesy of the Rakow Library of the Corning Museum of Glass.*

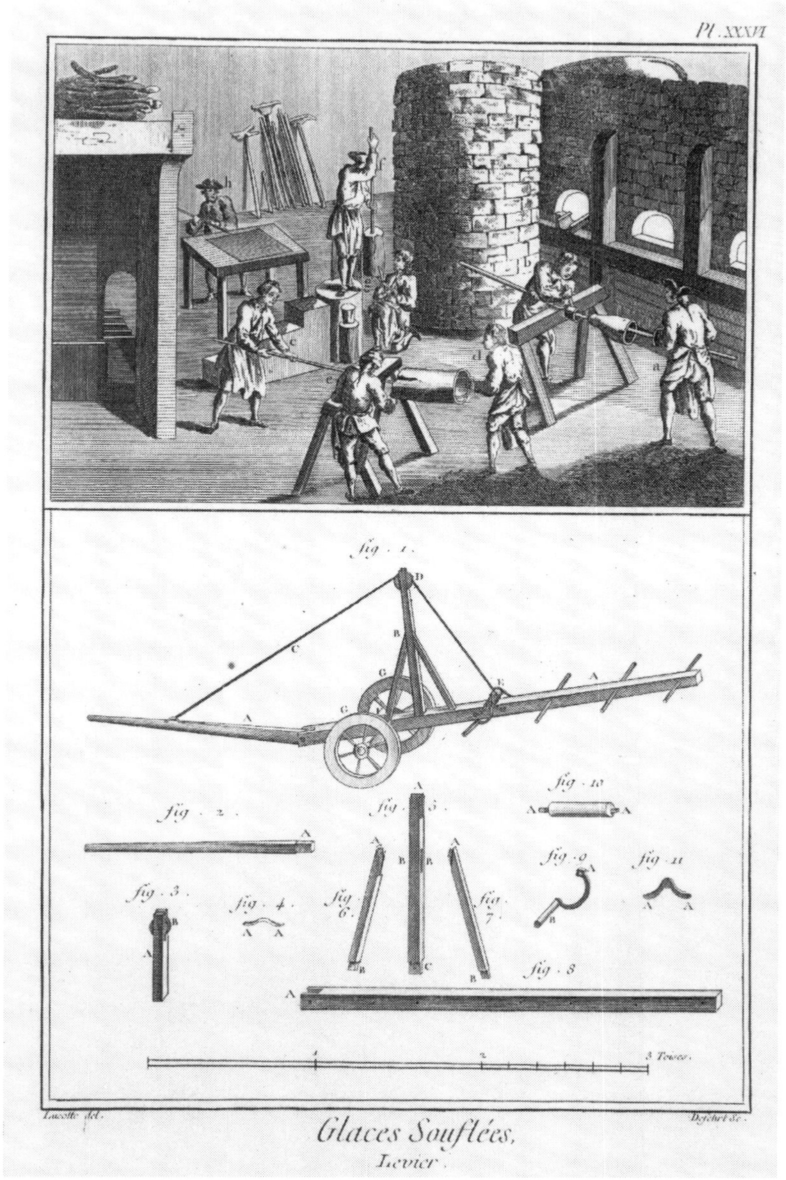

Figure 1.19 *Detail of annealing phase of cylinder method of making glass. Glass is placed in ovens and allowed to cool very slowly. From* Encyclopedie *by Denis Diderot, 18th century. Courtesy of the Rakow Library of the Corning Museum of Glass.*

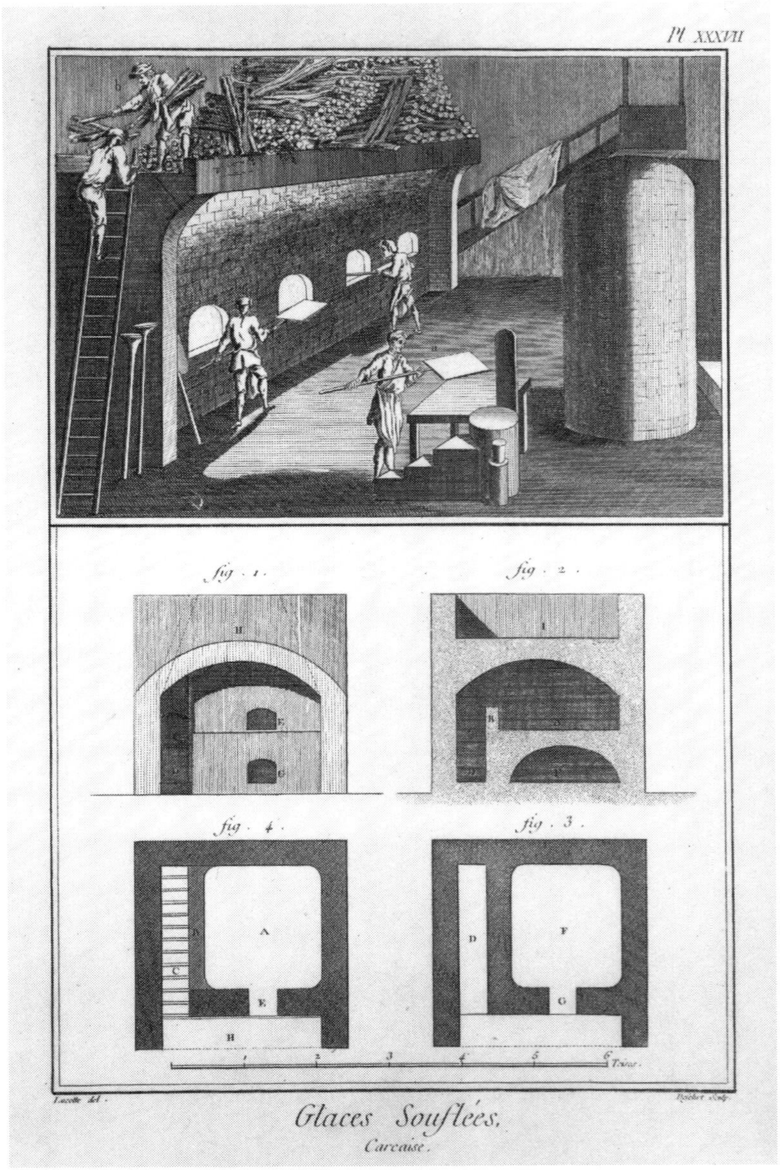

paper. Then, carefully slipping the paper out from under the glass with one hand, the glass came into direct contact with the amalgam. After being weighted, the glass emerged a bright, sparkling mirror. At this time, the maximum practical size for mirrors was about 30 inches wide and 45 inches in length (Goldberg, p. 140).

During the 16th and 17th centuries, hand mirrors were very popular for men and women, often found dangling from waists by ribbon, or attached to a fan. The French moralist Jean des Caurres complained in 1575 about the moral decay about him. "Alas! what an age we live in to see such depravity as we see, that induces them even to bring into church these scandalous mirrors hanging about their waist!" (Goldberg, p. 143). By the end of the century, the mirror would assume a less obvious form and be enclosed in what looked just like a simple little prayer book.

Books and broadsides of the time contain charming illustrations showing how varied attitudes were toward the mirror. The mirror could connote vanity and that which was false, since the reality in the mirror was a false reality. It was a common symbol for foolishness. In *This present boke named the Shyp of Folys* of 1509, a youth stands next to a fool who is gazing into a handheld mirror. A male cook stirs a pot. His attention is focused on his reflection as seen in a handheld looking glass.

However, the mirror can also symbolize agreeable traits. Since it is possible to look beyond oneself in a mirror and see a distant view, prudence and foresight are common attributes of the mirror. In *The English Gentleman and the English Gentlewoman*, 1641, a woman representing decency is seated in a chair holding a mirror. Mirrors were also important love emblems. In *A collection of Emblemes*, 1635, a woman looks into a mirror. Below the illustration is the phrase, "In all thine actions, have a care, that no unseemliness appear." As the woman looks into the glass to make sure her appearance will please her lover, so men should examine their actions in the glass of moral law. Additionally, a mirror was a useful tool to assist with working at a desk.

Mirrors were, at this time, also an important tool for scientific investigation. Leonardo da Vinci, one of civilization's great geniuses, was disappointed that his art was not as realistic as that which was shown in a mirror. He felt that painting should, in essence, be a mirror of reality. He also advised artists to "take a mirror and set it so that it reflects the actual things, then compare the reflection with your picture" (Goldberg, p. 152).

Venetian glassworks dominated European markets in the 16th century not only in mirrors, but also in glass for spectacles, medical and scientific apparatus, and decorative tableware. In addition to clear glass, Venetian glassware sometimes contained elaborate twisted patterns of clear and colored glass canes and sophisticated blown-glass animal forms. "Some gullible people believed that the best Venetian drinking glasses would shatter instantly should they come in contact with even a drop of poison—more a sign, perhaps, of the conspiratorial character of the times than of the nature of the material" (Zerwick, p. 51).

As early as 1599, Catherine de Medici had a "mirror room," which contained "one hundred and nineteen Venice mirrors set in the paneling" (Roche, p. 23).

The mirror room was an important development in 17th-century France and elsewhere. However, Venice was the major supplier. As other nations sought Venetian glassmaking secrets, conspiracies were rampant. In the middle of the century, Colbert, Louis XIV's finance minister, was incensed at the amount of money France was spending on imported mirrors and glassware. Intending to increase French production, in 1664 he instructed the French ambassador to Venice to hire some glassworkers from Murano. Fearful of retaliation, the workers were initially hesitant. Eventually, four workers were smuggled from Murano to France, where they were set up in a company started by Nicholas du Noyer. Another covert mission brought an additional 10 workers. The French incursions and intrigue infuriated Venetian authorities, who threatened to punish relatives of the workers. Additionally, Venetians fomented an armed insurrection among the workers. Two of the best workers died mysteriously, possibly by poison. The intrigue unnerved most of the workers, who, within two years, were repatriated to Venice with substantial monetary offers and signed pardons. In that short time, however, the damage had been done. "By 1671 few mirrors were any longer imported from Venice and all the king's needs were supplied by Noyer's company. A true devotee, Louis XIV set the fashion for mirrors. He purchased 700 of them in 1672" (Goldberg, p. 167). Noyer was given an exclusive 25-year right to produce mirrors, window glass, and other glass products. Noyer and his associates had privileges in the royal court, and the porters wore royal liveries. Noyer's company was named Saint Gobain after the village in which it was located, and has thrived to this day.

Other countries imported Venetian technology. Eventually, hundreds of Venetian glassworkers settled throughout Europe, often with similar stories of intrigue. Assassins were known to follow escaping glassworkers to the gates of Prague. The dominant force in mirror making, however, was by the end of the 17th century, France.

The French Influence

With government encouragement and growing demand from the aristocracy, the quantity and quality of glass products increased. A method of casting plate glass was developed by Bernard Perrot in 1673; he received a royal patent for his invention. Improvements in technology continued. Abraham Thevart, in 1688, developed a method of casting larger sheets of glass, 84 inches high and 50 inches wide. Haudicquer de Blancourt, in *The Art of Glass*, pointed out the importance of glass and mirrors to architecture and interior design at the end of the 17th century. He wrote,

> *Churches, palaces, castles and particular houses owe their chief ornaments as well as conveniences to glass; for that transparent substance guards them within from too great heat and cold, without hindering the intromission of the light. Looking-glasses, and other great plates of glasses are as so many surprising objects to our eyes, representing so distinctly and naturally all even from the least to the greatest Actions of the Objects before them; whereby also one may always keep himself in a neat and agreeable dress. Notwithstanding not one in a thousand of those who have them ever reflect on the admirableness of the work, which is beyond doubt, one of the chiefest and most perfect pieces of Art, and than which Man can make nothing more wonderful.* (de Blancourt, p. 5) (See Figure 1.20.)

The Hall of Mirrors was the most influential of the great mirror galleries in Europe. It was designed by Jules Hardouin-Mansart and Charles Le Brun and constructed between 1678 and 1686 for Louis XIV at Versailles, as part of a major enlargement of Versailles. Mirrors, sized approximately 2 feet by 3 feet 6 inches, separated by gold muntins, were elegantly installed into the arcade opposite the glass windows. According to Jean-Marie Perouse, "Hardouin-Mansart was probably responsible for the overall design, which features pilasters similar to those in his celebrated gallery at the chateau of Clagny (destroyed). In all likelihood he was also responsible for the decision to use mirror revetments. Such facings had been fashionable since the middle of the century, but Mansart may also have been drawn to them because they minimized the surface available to the painter, who was a rival"(Perouse, p. 57). In spite of any artistic rivalry, one assumes that the opportunity to reflect the enormous formal pools and gardens beyond the terrace, and the ability to reflect additional sunlight, must have swayed the designers in favor of the mirrors. The mirrors also reflected silver furniture, torchieres, and candelabra as well as the spectacular life of the French court. They were located in the central suite, which provided the primary access to the king's bedroom.

Figure 1.20 *A print celebrating glass and mirror products, "Habit de Marchand Miroitier Lunettier," c. 1700, Germany, G. Valck, publisher. Courtesy of the Rakow Library of the Corning Museum of Glass.*

Although the Hall of Mirrors was spectacular and, literally, the center of court life at Versailles, other magnificent installations of mirror abound in that enormous palace. The Salon of War, the Room of the Bull's-Eye, and the King's Bedroom all use mirror in large scale, architectural fashion.

Versailles set the fashion for mirrors and mirror galleries throughout Europe. Among some of the most important were the Hotel de la Vrillière in Paris; the palace of Stockholm; Schonbrunn; Charlottenburg; and the Residence at Stuttgart of 1753. In Russia, Peter the Great created a new city in the style of Versailles, St. Petersburg. Catherine the Great bought hundreds of works of art and furnishings, and had mirrors installed in the French fashion. The Amalienburg Pavilion in Munich, designed by Francois Cuvillies, a Flemish-born designer who had studied in France, combined mirrors and rococo ornamentation (see Figure 1.21).

A vocabulary of mirror design began to develop. As at Versailles, mirrors were often placed opposite windows in order to amplify the existing daylight. They were often placed between windows in the form of *pier mirrors*. Pier mirrors made the massive outer walls seem less heavy. In architecturally awkward spaces, they were particularly useful. If, for instance, there were only two windows along a wall with an intervening pier, a mirror on the pier would help to dematerialize it and make it less noticeable.

Another important location for the mirror was over fireplaces. Called the *overmantel mirror*, it was useful in imparting a brightness to a portion of the room in which there were invariably no windows. During the time of Louis XIV the large overmantel mirror, built into the architecture, was termed "au royale." In the king's bedroom, one such mirror reflects the ornate bed and the bust of the king. In 1737, the designer J. F. Blondel mentioned in some of his writings that the fireplace was the most important area in a room on which to concentrate decoration. He noted that mirrors would make the best impression, since they were expensive, particularly if one did not have a great deal of money to spend (see Figure 1.22).

In mirror rooms, tremendous creativity with mirrors ensued. Mirrors were set in panels in varied shapes; occasionally, they were faceted; they were set into panels in ceilings; sometimes columns were mirrored; and they were often used in displays of porcelain, Delft ware and figurines.

As the quality of mirrors improved and the size of the panes increased, mirrors were often placed opposite other mirrors. This created the effect called *glaces à repetitions*. Invariably, there was a chandelier placed between the mirrors so that when the candles were lit, there was an expansion of light into infinity rather than darkness. The chandelier compen-

Figure 1.21 *Amalienburg Pavilion, Nymphenburg Park, Munich, Germany, 18th century. Design by Francois Cuvillies. Photo by Sandak. Courtesy of Schloss Nymphenburg.*

Figure 1.22 *Mantel design by Daniel Marot, from his* Uvres contenant plussieurs penseez, *1700. Courtesy of the Library of Congress, Rare Book Division.*

sated for the naturally greenish tinge of the glass in mirrors that would be intensified when reflected ad infinitum.

As society changed in France, naturally, tastes changed as well. The Baroque grandeur of Louis XIV gave way to Regency, rococo, and neoclassic styles, moving into the Napoleonic era. Other countries established mirror-making industries and created mirrors for their own cultures. England and Ireland created magnificent framed mirrors, which they exported to America. Initially, American industry was stymied by taxation because of British mercantilistic ideas that sought raw materials in the colonies, yet used them as markets for their finished products.

By the 19th century, even though different styles had emerged, the vocabulary of mirror design that had originated in the early palaces would now be replicated in hotels, restaurants, cafes, and departments stores. The mirror that had once been available for the nobility exclusively was now available to anyone.

America

With the arrival of English settlers came numerous failed attempts at glassmaking. In 1608, a group of six glassblowers was included in the early settlement at Jamestown in order to start a glass factory. The ready stores of timber and sand appealed to investors. At that time, English glass manufacturers were forbidden to use timber in glassmaking because it was marked for the shipbuilding industry. However, the Jamestown facility failed due to local hardships, the quarrelsome nature of the glassmakers and the great distance to the foreign markets. Other attempts at glassmaking were made at Salem, in Philadelphia, and in New Amsterdam, but all failed. Finally, in 1739, Frederick Wistar started a glass factory in southern New Jersey using German glassblowers. The Wistar factory defied official British policy, which required America to provide raw materials for British factories and ready markets for their finished products. For most of the 18th and early 19th centuries, mirrors were imported from England and France, and were highly prized due to their rarity and cost. The imported mirrors were usually smaller and far less elaborate than their counterparts in England and Europe. American interiors used framed mirrors rather than mirrors installed in paneling in the French style. Design books of Thomas Chippendale, Sheraton, Hepplewhite, and others guided craftsmen in this country (see Figure 1.23).

The 19th century saw improvements in glass and mirror manufacturing and a greater availability of these products for the expanding middle class (see Figure 1.24). In the

***Figure 1.23** Frame design from the first Chippendale design book,* Gentleman and Cabinet-makers Director, *1754. Few American craftsmen had the ability to re-create these elaborate conceptions in wood. Courtesy of the Library of Congress, Rare Book Division.*

1840s, for example, Justus von Liebig, a German chemist, improved the reflective coating of mirrors by pouring a liquid solution of silver directly onto the glass.

The Beaux Arts period gave Americans some of the grand mirror installations in the French style in mansions and public buildings in the major cities. Different approaches regarding mirrors emerged in the 1920s and 1930s. Gone were the ornate frames of the Beaux Arts. Instead, walls of mirror were used. One New York entrance hall had walls lined with mirror, on which were painted skyscrapers and airplanes. The round frameless mirror looked new in its traditional location, over a simplified mantel (see Figure 1.25).

Figure 1.24 Woman in a Victorian Interior, *E. L. Henry, 1890. Courtesy of the New York State Museum, Albany.*

Figure 1.25 *Apartment of Katherine Brush, New York.*
Design: Joseph Urban, 1933. Photo: Fay S. Lincoln.
Courtesy of Architectural Record.

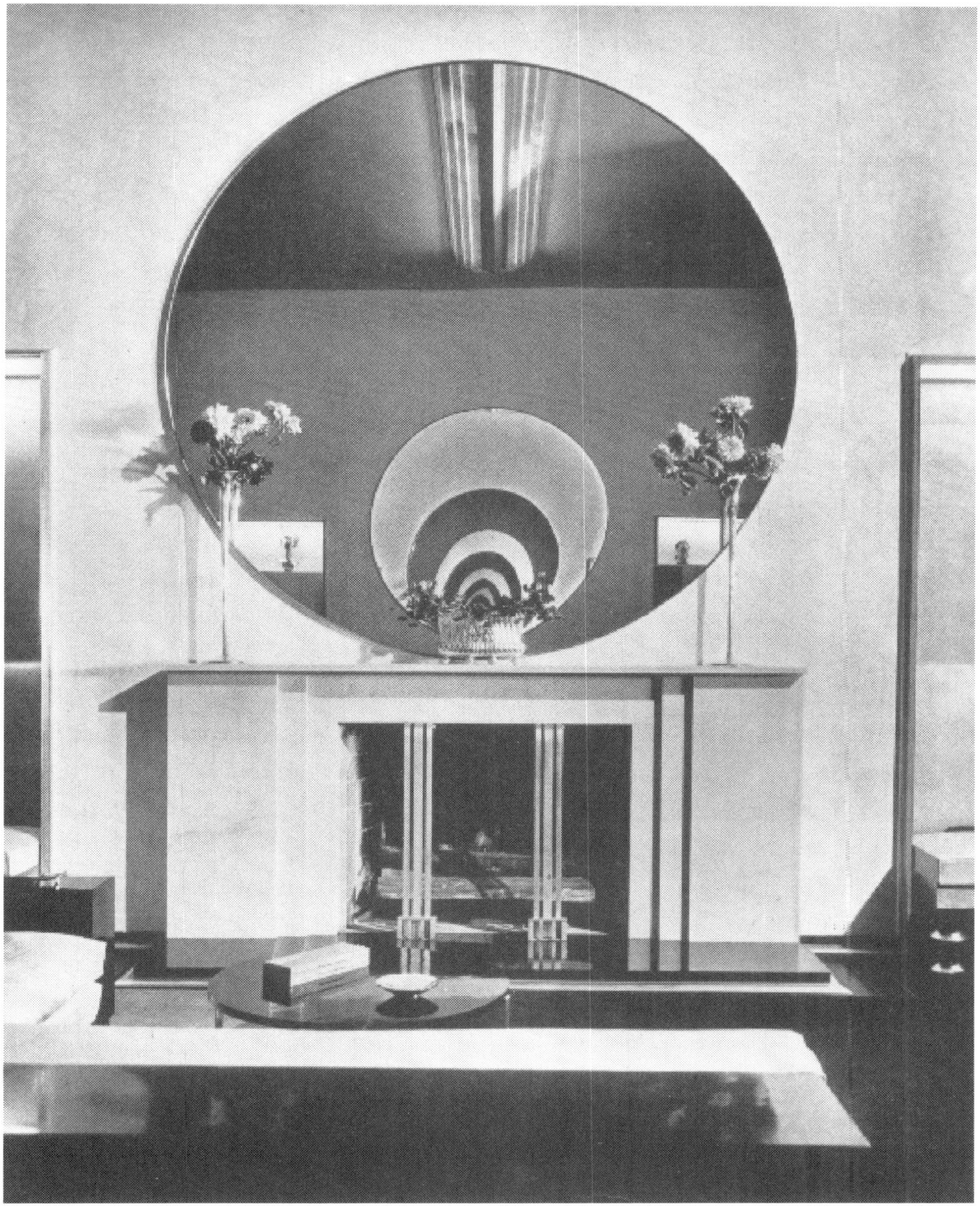

With the repeal of Prohibition in 1933, bars and restaurants suddenly had to appeal to women, something the turn-of-the-century saloons did not have to do to attract patrons. Articles in design magazines instructed architects that the new feminine clientele would demand novelty surface treatments, powder rooms, and mirrors. With the Depression and World War II, however, not much building occurred, and the use of mirrors declined as well.

During this period, however, Hollywood, the producer of celluloid illusions, used the mirror in a creative fashion to give the audience glamorous interiors as well as psychological insight in a way never before possible on stage. The movie *Rebecca* uses a mirrored dressing table set amidst 30-foot-high billowing draperies as the symbol of the dead, beautiful, and mysterious Rebecca. The bleak mood of *Citizen Kane* is intensified in one of the final scenes by an image of mirrors placed opposite each other in a hallway, resulting in darkness cascading into infinity. In *All about Eve*, multiple reflections are cynically amusing as the latest ingenue, wearing her rival's robe and crown, bows to the multiple mirrors.

But in architecture, as the International Style took hold after World War II, the interest in the mirror waned. The mirror, which had been so successful in dematerializing mass, was no match for the glass windows that dematerialized it in the new skyscrapers. Although mirror-like materials, such as dark marble or chrome on furniture, were in evidence, the mirror itself was less visible.

In the 1960s and 1970s, the hippie culture loosened American attitudes. Bright colors, reflective surfaces—often looking like fun-house mirrors—and trompe l'oeil were popular. The Miesien dictum of "less is more" was modified by Robert Venturi to "less is a bore." People were getting tired of the coldness of the steel-and-glass building.
Ironically, at this time, one of the most austere architectural forms was being developed: the all-mirror building, also known as the mirror-glass building. In the hands of sensitive designers, it reflected grass, trees, sky, and clouds. In the hands of more commercial architects, parking lots and freeways were part of the reflections. Additionally, the all-mirror building sometimes assumed an impersonal scalelessness.

Transparent mirror for office buildings originated in the late 1950s, evolving from the curtain-wall building. When Eero Saarinen and Associates were working on the General Motors Technical Institute at the start of the 1950s, they were aware of the problems with all glass buildings in terms of heat buildup. They did not want to use venetian blinds and tinted glass, though. At the end of the decade, John Dinkeloo, then a partner in the firm, began to investigate the possibility of developing a glass that could reflect light—and, therefore, heat—away from the building before it ever entered the wall. He thought that the one-way mirror could be developed for architectural use on the outside of buildings. At that time, the one-way mirror was used primarily for observation rooms in hospitals and police stations.

The architects sought a more durable material than the one-way mirrors that could be easily scratched. Working with Kinney Glass, a small glass company, the architects developed a new product, consisting of the electrolytic deposition of metal on glass in a vacuum chamber. In order to protect the metal film, a second piece of glass was laminated to the back. The first building to utilize the new glass was Bell Labs in Holmdel, New Jersey, which was finished in 1962 (see Figure 1.26).

Kevin Roche, who carried on the Saarinen firm after the death of Eero Saarinen, has used the material on the exterior of buildings, such as on angled sun shades rather than simply in vertical surfaces. He has used it in decorative ways on interiors as well. He has designed tables with mirror-glass tops and wall panels with variations in lighting to exploit the material's transparency and reflectivity.

Figure 1.26 *First mirror-glass building: Bell Labs, Holmdel, NJ. Design: Eero Saarinen, 1962. Courtesy of Bell Labs.*

In the 1970s and 1980s, other architects began to explore different aspects of mirror's ability to shade glass or to create solar energy. Gunnar Birkerts' Corning Museum of Glass features a large-scale periscope placed on the exterior of the building. The view is cast upward from a lower canted mirrored spandrel to the upper "eyebrow," which also acts as a sunshade (see Figure 1.27).

Figure 1.27 *Periscope installed on the exterior of a building. Corning Museum of Glass, Corning, NY. Design: Gunnar Birkerts and Associates, Inc., 1980.*

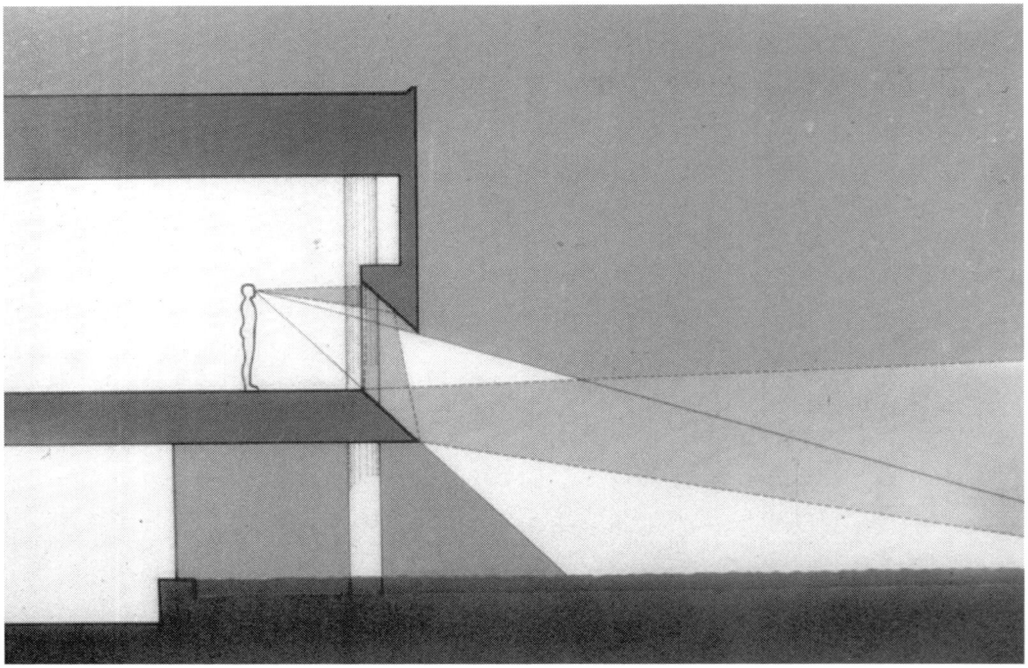

James Lambeth's Colorado ski lodge took the same mirror glass that had been used on office buildings and installed it in an arc, relating to solar angles. The canted window was used to melt snow on the door stoop of the ski lodge (see Figure 1.28). A material that had been designed to make office buildings cooler now took that heat and focused it.

Figure 1.28 *Yocum Lodge with canted mirror glass over entrance used to melt snow. Design: James Lambeth, 1972.*

Recent Developments in Mirror Fabrication

In the 19th and 20th centuries, blown-glass and plate-glass processes became more automated. Large cylinders were created with compressed air, then slit and flattened. Plate glass continued to be made with large-scale grinding devices. Then, in 1959, Pilkington Brothers, an English corporation, introduced a float-glass process, which was a radical departure from the blown- and cast-glass processes of the past. Molten glass was poured on a bed of liquid tin and spread to form a wide, flat ribbon of glass. This eliminated the cumbersome grinding of the past and revolutionized glass production. PPG introduced the Pilkington process to the United States in 1963, with subsequent refinements of its own. By 1979, PPG had discontinued its traditional methods of manufacturing sheet and plate glass to focus exclusively on the float-glass process.

Whereas glass for cookware, containers, and lighting equipment are blown, pressed, or molded, float glass is manufactured in wide continuous ribbons. Raw materials are gathered from silos and carefully blended, then inserted into the melting furnace in a precisely calibrated environment. A typical float-glass furnace has a melting area about 165 feet long, 30 feet wide, and 4 feet deep, and holds approximately 1,500 tons of molten glass. The batch enters the tank at the charging end and is melted at about 2800 degrees Fahrenheit. Flowing out of the melting furnace, it enters the forming chamber onto the perfectly flat bed of molten tin. The speed of the flow, or draw, in the tank determines the thickness of the glass. Generally, the slower the flow, the thicker the glass. Molten glass leaves the melting furnace and flows into a float bath, an oblong tank that is 160 feet long and wide enough to carry the widest standard commercial size of glass.

The float bath is divided into three zones. In the first zone, heat from the molten tin and top heater causes the glass to float uniformly over the flat surface, thus creating a ribbon of glass with parallel surfaces. The second zone gives the glass an exceptionally brilliant finish. The third, or cooling zone, maintains the perfect flatness and transparency of the glass until it is sufficiently hard to be conveyed to the rollers in the annealing oven, or *lehr*. Precise control of heat along the length of the float bath is required.

In the annealing lehr, the temperature of the glass is lowered through different temperature zones, from approximately 1200 degrees F to 400 degrees F to control the stresses and strains that would occur if the glass were cooled too quickly. From the cooling area, the glass is washed and moved to the warehouse for inspection, cutting, and final shipment to the mirror manufacturer.

Making Mirror

When the glass arrives from the supplier, it is washed and electronically inspected to detect even the slightest scratch or flaw. A solution of tin is applied to the surface of the glass, then washed off. This gives the surface an adhesion quality for silvering. Then, approximately 18 coats of pure silver are sprayed onto the glass.

The silver must be sealed, or, like ordinary silver in the home, it will tarnish. It is sealed by an application of a copper coating using electrolysis (a process that employs copper sulfate to deposit the copper on the silver). This is often called a "sacrificial coating," since the copper is simply sacrificed to protect the more valuable silver. Then, a tough durable enamel is applied to the copper to protect it from oxidizing and to prevent the silver from separating. It is baked on at 250 degrees to assure a hard, flexible finish.

Newer processes include sputtering—which is the application of reflective coatings in a vacuum chamber—and pyrolytic coatings—silicons and metal oxides applied while the glass is still molten. The effect of these developments is to give the designer a tremendous assortment of mirrored products from which to choose.

Mirrored Products

Clear mirror: Glass with silver backing, copper and paint. It has four standard thicknesses today: 3⁄32", 1⁄8", 3⁄16", and 1⁄4". Quarter inch is generally used for all applications with thinner mirrors used in conjunction with furniture. The largest standard size is 65" x 84", but custom sizes are possible.

Although the glass has a slightly greenish tinge, most people do not find it objectionable.

Pyrolytic mirror: While the glass is approximately 1,200° F (a dull red color), it receives a chemical vapor deposition of silicon and metal oxides. Slightly less reflective than silver mirror, pyrolytic mirror has advantages for the designer in that it does not corrode in wet or salt atmospheres, and can be tempered after fabrication. Libbey-Owens-Ford markets its pyrolytic product as Mirage.

Tinted mirror: The glass itself is tinted a variety of colors, including gold, pink, peach, green, blue, bronze, gray, and black.

Transparent mirror: This type of mirror is made of clear glass with, typically, a 60 percent reflective coating on the back of the glass. The coating might be chrome or titanium instead of silver.

Safety mirror: This type of mirror has vinyl tape on the back, which is cut to the size of the glass. An example would be a shower door that would look like a mirror on the room side but like a painted surface on the shower side. The purpose of the vinyl backing is to hold the glass together should a person fall against the glass. This is the most cost-effective form of safety glass. Two layers of tape can be provided depending on code requirements.

Figure 1.29 *"Antique Mirror." Courtesy of Carolina Mirror.*

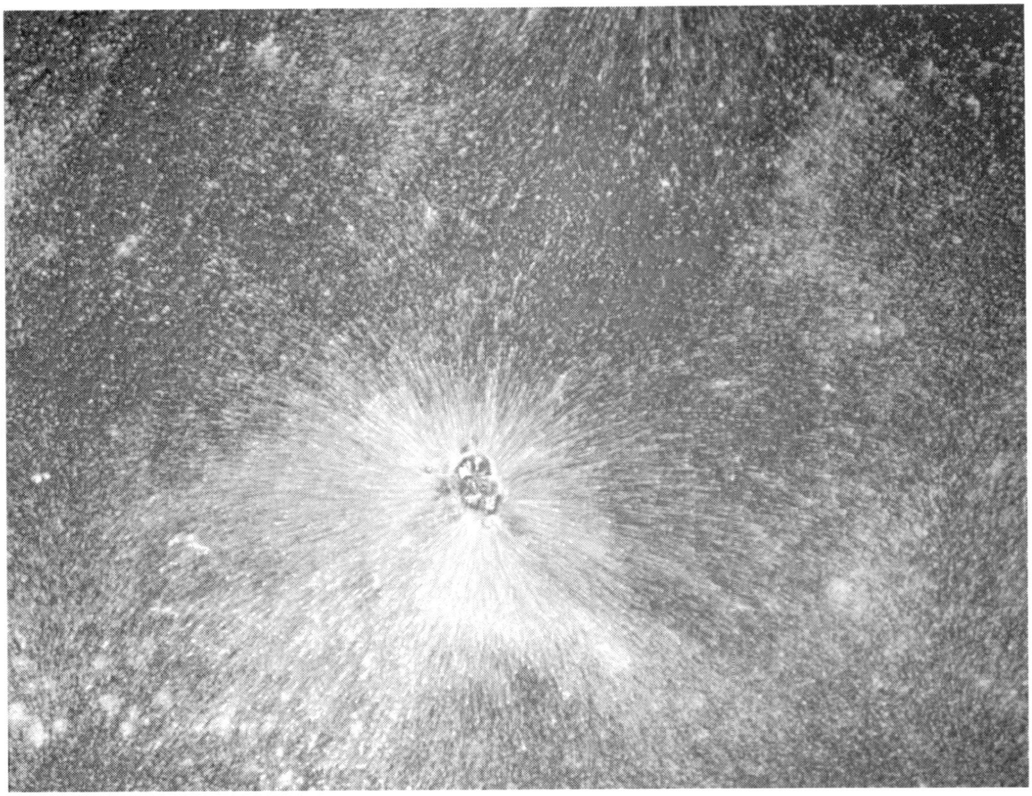

Tempered mirror: Clear glass is heated a second time in ovens and becomes tempered. Silver is then deposited on the glass. The advantage is that the glass, if broken, will break into pellets, like a car window. The disadvantages are that the glass is not perfectly flat; hence, distortions will occur in the mirror. It is also an expensive procedure.

Low-iron mirror or Starphire™: Also called ultra-clear mirror, this is the clearest of all mirrors. Since it has lower iron content than most glass, it does not have the greenish tint of clear mirror. It has a slightly blue tint, noticeable on the edge.

Antiqued mirrors: These products can look like old mercury mirrors that have theoretically been worn away with moisture. Some contain new color ranges and have wide variations in aesthetic possibilities, looking anything but antique (see Figure 1.29).

Plastic mirror: This is softer and easier to bend and scratch than glass. It is coated with metals. It is used for crafts, display, and children's furniture and toys.

Metal mirror: Used for occasional areas where utmost security is demanded.

First-surface mirrors: These are optical mirrors for cameras and kaleidoscopes. They are occasionally used by artists and designers. The problem with first-surface mirrors is fragility.

Surface Treatments

Sandblasting: Glass will receive a clouded surface, usually to result in a pattern. The cloudy surface can be applied either to the front of the mirror or to the rear. Application to the rear results in the removal of some of the reflective coating and backing paints (see Figure 1.30). This is often used to allow light to penetrate the glass (see Figure 1.31).

Cutting: Miter cutting or abrading done with wheels on the front or rear surface of the glass (see Figure 1.32).

Carving: Multi-level effects created with abrasives and high-pressure air sources. If applied on the rear, the pattern is typically painted, sometimes in varying colors (see Plate 4).

Acid etching: This is used in Europe, less so in the United States. Acid creates patterns in the glass, which can then be painted (see Figure 1.33).

Painted: Designs can be painted onto the front surface of the mirror. Floral patterns were popular in the 19th century. The rear of mirrors can also be painted. This can be in the form of images, or a smooth lacquer.

Laminating: Two or more pieces of glass can be brought together with a vinyl interlayer. Various films, patterns, or materials can be introduced. Laminated glass can be silvered.

Coating: Many coatings can be applied to glass with effects ranging from translucent to iridescent, such as dichroic coatings.

Slumping: Glass can be heated, then cast in a mold, then silvered.

Texturing: Various textures can be created in glass which is then silvered.

Glue chipping: A special glue is applied to the glass. When it dries, flakes of glass come off in a frost pattern. It can then be silvered.

Edge Treatments

Smoothing: Results in a safe pencil or radiused edge.

Polished edge: Results in greater brilliance of edge.

Beveling: Of various thicknesses depending on the thickness of the glass, beveling can be quite decorative.

Figure 1.30 *Example of sandblasting in a scroll pattern. Courtesy of Saint-Gobain.*

Figure 1.31 *Example of a sandblasted store logo. Courtesy of Saint-Gobain.*

Figure 1.32 *Example of a cut pattern. Courtesy of Saint-Gobain.*

Figure 1.33 *An acid-etched mirror with clear and painted patterns on the back surface of the mirror. The etching is done prior to silvering. Courtesy of Sekon Glassworks, Ltd., London. Photo: John Simmonds.*

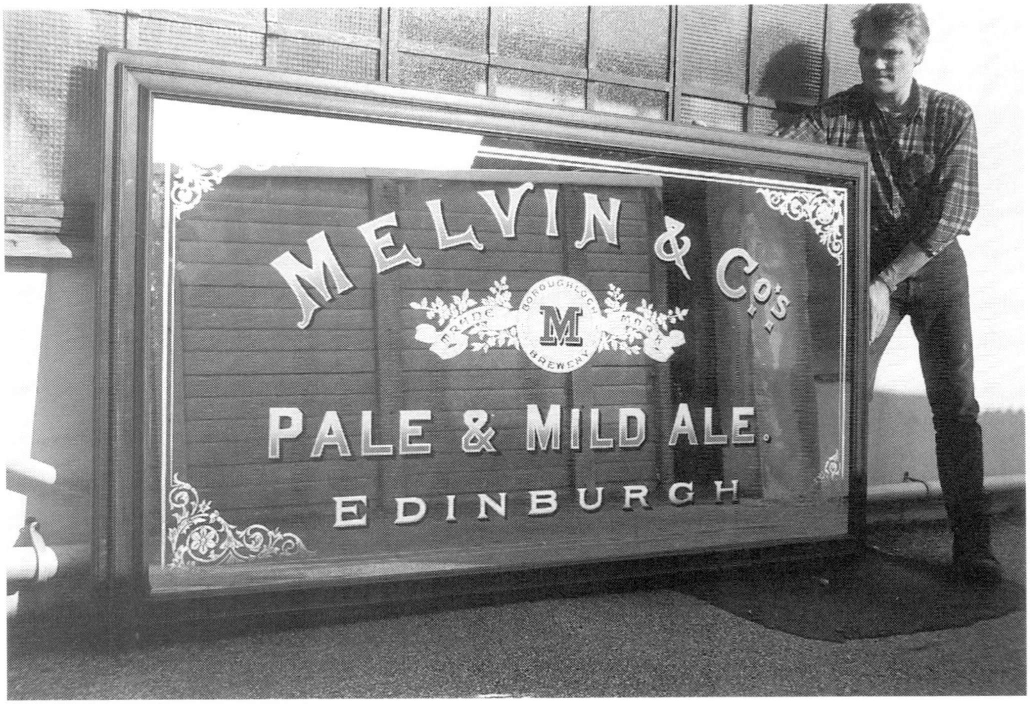

Mirror by Design

Now that we have seen something about how mirrors are made, how they work, and their history, it is time to look at how many designers, past and present, have used mirror—by design. We will look at aesthetic and philosophical approaches, along with some technical advice pertaining to support, attachment, moisture control, and cleaning.

The following sections will move from the least illusionary mirrors to the most illusionary mirrors. Our least illusionary mirror is the one we look into every morning in our bath and dressing areas. We will look at ramifications of "The Person in the Mirror." Then we will look at framed mirrors, mirrored screens, mirrored furniture, and mirror that we recognize as mirror: "The Mirrored Accent." Next, we will see increasingly illusionary mirror applications in the section on "Space." In some of these instances, the designers will have boosted the mirror's illusionary qualities to such an extent that the mirror has all but disappeared as a finite object. Finally, in "The Dynamic Mirror" we will see view shifting, casting sunlight into remote regions, periscoping, and using the mirror as a device for solar energy. Sunlight dappling the walls in an atrium might be cast by mirrors, but the occupants often won't know, nor will they care. In this case, the mirror has truly disappeared from consciousness.

The organization of the following sections of the book, while moving from least illusionary to most illusionary mirrors, also parallels the mirror's history. We have seen how the mirror moved from a handheld object, to a decorative accent, and to larger sheets with greater spatial implications. Finally, we have seen the experiments of shifting views, sunlight, and focusing energy in large-scale ways with mirrors. The burning mirror of the past is now a scientific experiment in outer space.

Obviously, categorizing images is often a value judgment. Many uses of the mirror overlap. The mirror that conveys space can also reflect our faces and can also redirect sunlight. And there will always be variables that cross the mirror's surface. Those variables certainly add to the intrigue of the mirror. Who cannot gaze at the grand salons at Versailles and not wonder about the past spectacles and entertainments that appeared briefly in those same mirrors?

However, the variables usually do not constitute a beautiful use of mirror. The variables reflected in the mirrors at Versailles today are us, casually dressed tourists carrying guidebooks and cameras. The mirrors are beautiful, however, because of their detailing and their magnificent architectural setting that they have reflected for more than 300 years.

2

The Person in the Mirror

"There was never yet fair woman but she made mouths in a glass."
(Shakespeare, King Lear, Act II, Scene 2)

Here's looking at you!

We probably do not realize how much we look at ourselves in the mirror throughout the day. Is any of us brave enough to leave the house in the morning without a peek in the mirror? Today, the mirror is essential to grooming and dressing, and is omnipresent in exercise areas, lobbies, and places of leisure. Not only do we observe ourselves in the mirror, but we use it to observe others as well.

An acquaintance mentioned that in her puritanical childhood, the only mirror allowed in the home was a small bathroom mirror. This is a rare attitude in society today. Our children are typically brought up with houses full of mirrors. Even our cities are filled with mirrors, in store windows and on mirror-glass buildings, which are clad with transparent mirrors. An office worker once recounted being at his desk on the ground floor of a mirror-glass building. He noted with amusement that women would come by and primp in the windows, since the windows seemed to be mirrors from the outside.

We have at our disposal a wide variety of mirror products, ranging from clear and ultra-clear mirror to tinted and transparent mirror; fog-free mirrors; concave, dome, and convex mirrors; and the "true mirror," which corrects for the mirror's reversal.

How do we show ourselves in the best light in mirrors in the various environments in which they are likely to occur? And what are the psychological implications of using mirror? Babies love mirrors and develop faster with them present. Sometimes it is important to see ourselves. Sometimes we do not want to be reminded of the passage of time and our inevitable aging processes. Lighting and the appropriate kind and placement of mirror are very important where the reflection of the human is involved. The discussion of the mirror that reflects the person will focus on three distinct areas:

1. *The personal realm:* Bathing, dressing, exercise areas and bedrooms. Here, the mirror helps us with basic grooming necessities, helps us stay in shape, and perhaps helps us revive our spirits and relax.
2. *The public realm:* Most of us appreciate the opportunity to check on our appearances in places of transition, such as foyers and lobbies, shops, and public exercise areas. Mirrors can also make dining a much more pleasant experience psychologically.
3. *Specialized uses:* Mirrors are important in child care settings, both for the caregiver to check on the child, and for the child to develop self-awareness and to enhance motor skills. Convex mirrors are important here, as well as in corridors, in shops, and near cash machines. Tilted mirrors are useful for those in wheelchairs.

As has been noted, there are always overlapping uses with the mirror. Large mirrors are popular in bathrooms, since we can see more than just our faces in them. They are also popular because of increasing light and spatial amplification. Richard Neutra, one of the few international-style architects to use mirror, wrote, "The smallest interior like a bathroom benefits most from reflective walls which seem to recede into depth unavailable in the floor plan."

Background

Early mirrors were used for scrying, to create fires, as artifacts for statues of gods, and as grooming aids, especially for women. Whether made from stone, bronze, gold, or silver—

and, later, glass and silver—their prime focus was the face, especially the face of a woman. Rembrandt's often somber self-portraits were painted with the aid of a mirror. Yet, when the mirror was an attribute in a painting, it was most often with a woman looking into it.

Plutarch, the Greek moralist, wrote, somewhat ungallantly, of the essential role of the mirror in the feminine quest for beauty.

> *If you saw women getting out of bed in the morning, you would find them more repulsive than monkeys. That is why they shut themselves up and refuse to be seen by a man; old hags and a troupe of servant maids as ugly as their mistress surround her, plastering her unhappy face with a variety of medicaments. For a woman does not just wash away her sleepiness with cold water, and proceed to a serious day's work. No, innumerable concoctions in the way of salves are used to brighten her unpleasing complexion. As in a public procession, each of the servants has some different object in her hand; a silver basin, a jug, a mirror, a multitude of boxes, enough to stock a chemist's shop, jars full of mischief, tooth powders or stuff for blackening the eyelids.* (Balsdon, p. 255)

In an account by Juvenal, a mistress, angered by a mistake with her coiffure by a slave was depicted as "attacking the girl's face with her nails, seizing her arms and scratching them with her very sharp-pointed hair pins, tearing her hair, or thrashing her with a mirror" (Balsdon, p. 255). The mistress would typically have used a metal mirror with a handle. In a society where a woman's future and social standing were often dependent on her appearance, the mirror was a necessary, and sometimes cruel, ally.

Glass mirrors

As we have seen, the glass mirror took centuries to develop. Although the hand-held mirror has remained with us to this day, most find it more convenient to keep the hands free. In 18th-century France, glass mirrors were ingeniously incorporated into secretary/dressing tables that had movable tops with side compartments that opened as well. In the 19th century, bureaus were developed to store the greater accumulation of clothing. These might have had a small rotating mirror set on top, with its own small drawer at the base. Eventually, larger mirrors were added to the tops of the chests. The cheval mirror, a vertical mirror that could be rotated or placed on a stand, permitted view of the complete person.

Development of the bathroom

The ancient civilization of Crete had running water and flush toilets. Ancient Rome and medieval Europe had public baths. In spite of this, superstitions against bathing developed at various times. For instance, the courtiers at Versailles under Louis XIV rarely bathed.

Attitudes changed in the 18th century. A typical dressing room at that time might have mirrored panels, a movable metal bath, a portable closestool and wash stand. Even simple American farmhouses had their table with washbowl, jug for water, and small, wood-framed mirror hanging on the wall above.

The modern bathroom, as we know it, was a development of the 19th century. At the beginning of the 19th century, one of the most sumptuous baths of all time, that of Madame Beauharnais at the Hotel Beauharnais in Paris, was created. It featured multiple painted wood columns, marble inlay, and a metal interior in the tub. It had dim lighting, giving the room a mystery enhanced by the reflection of the columns in the distance. This was not a room for one superstitious about bathing or nervous about seeing herself reflected in the multiple mirrors (see Plate 6).

The Hotel Beauharnais bath was created exclusively for the enjoyment of a wealthy individual. Soon, however, products began to be mass produced. At the end of the 19th century, "fitted furniture" was developed, which could be ordered from catalogues. On one side of a fireplace might be a built-in washstand with a built-in mirror above it, and on the other side might be a dresser, with its identical mirror. Soon the paneling was eliminated, and cast iron tubs and porcelain sinks ruled. With the development of mass housing in the 20th century, the bathroom plan became standardized. From the 1920s through the 1950s, five feet by seven feet was the typical size of the bathroom, which contained one small sink, toilet, and bath/shower combination. Mirrors became increasingly important in those spaces.

Today, the powder room is no longer a luxury, but a necessity, especially if we want to resell our homes. We have fun decorating these rooms to show our individual tastes.

Many homes now have a bathroom for the children, and some even have one bath per child. The master bath is very often a sumptuous retreat. The bath, usually separate from the shower, frequently takes center stage. It might look out over a landscape, or be set into a mirror-lined niche. Decorative effects, such as flowers or swans sandblasted on mirror, are popular in bath areas.

The bath might face a double sink, containing a large expanse of mirror. The little medicine cabinet of times past has been overtaken by recessed, decorative, or high-tech medicine cabinets combined with lights. Some designers prefer creating customized storage columns, often combined with lights.

Do's and Don'ts when Using Mirror to Reflect People

Lighting: The proper type of lighting is determined by the function of the space. Bright, even lighting is best for grooming and shaving. Spotlights, though popular with designers since they are easy to specify, can cast deep shadows on the face. If spotlights are used, they should be supplemented with additional electric lighting or daylighting. The most flattering lighting for makeup application is the old-fashioned theatrical dressing room lights—incandescent lights running around the top and sides of the mirror. However, since this approach produces a great deal of heat and is energy-intensive, other solutions are recommended. Fluorescent lighting mounted behind the mirror or built into soffits or into luminous panels rimming the mirror can look sleekly contemporary and be energy-efficient and flattering, particularly if a warmer color of lamp is specified.

Dressing areas also benefit from even lighting. To be avoided are spotlights, which cast deep shadows on face and form, and cool white fluorescent overhead fixtures, which are almost universally unflattering.

Areas for bathing or relaxing can, of course, use dimmer, more variable lighting. The bathroom in the Hotel Beauharnais contains an example of a soft lighting fixture that is duplicated in the mirrors and does not shine into the eyes of the bath's occupant.

The most flattering light possible is a form that few of us today have experienced. That is the overhead chandelier filled with real candles. The soft flickering and glimmer of the candles, and the quality of light, cannot be replicated with electric lights. Even lights on a dimmer cannot create the same effect.

In a more modern vein, the television design personality, Kitty Bartholomew, recently interviewed a California designer who used large wax candles on one corner of her bathtub to create a relaxing environment. She let the wax run down the sides of the tub.

Color: Remember the importance of reflected light from adjacent walls, and the importance of reflected color on the person's face. Navy blue might be fine for a powder room where one will stay briefly; however, it is not appropriate for a bathroom where makeup or shaving are involved. Unless the intensity of the light is increased, the reflection in the mirror will contain blue shadows. Additionally, consider ultra-clear mirror for areas where shaving will be done or makeup applied.

Clutter: Do not forget how much clutter can be generated today, with hair-drying equipment and assorted cosmetic bottles and jars. Adequate storage is important to prevent these items from being doubled or quadrupled in the mirrors.

Remember the Law of Reflection

The law of reflection can be a boon or a bane.

The *triple mirror* is desirable in dressing rooms to show the person's side views (see Figure 2.1).

Two mirrors at a *right angle* are not appropriate for dressing rooms, as they will produce a split image in the corner. A woman who owned a bridal shop made this mistake and had to tear out the mirrors because the reflections were confusing. Although this is the basis of the "true mirror," that device is small and designed to show primarily the face, and it minimizes the objectionable joint since special first-surface mirrors are used.

Multiple reflections produced by multiple mirrors, such as mirrors en face, or opposite, will, of course, reflect the occupant of the space as well as the space itself. This can be unnerving on occasion.

Check the height of mirrors, and the height of fixtures (see Figure 2.2). A 6'2" man, for example, standing a comfortable distance from a bathroom mirror, will see the top of his head as being approximately four inches lower than it actually is; hence, a six-foot-high mirror will suffice in most situations. This happens to be the height recommended for the electric panel behind Mystic Mirror's "fog-free mirror," which uses electrical heat to eliminate condensation. Although the mirror itself may go to the ceiling, the panel only needs to be the height of the reflected image (see Figure 2.9).

Figure 2.1 *Triple mirror. Plan view of typical arrangement of panels.*

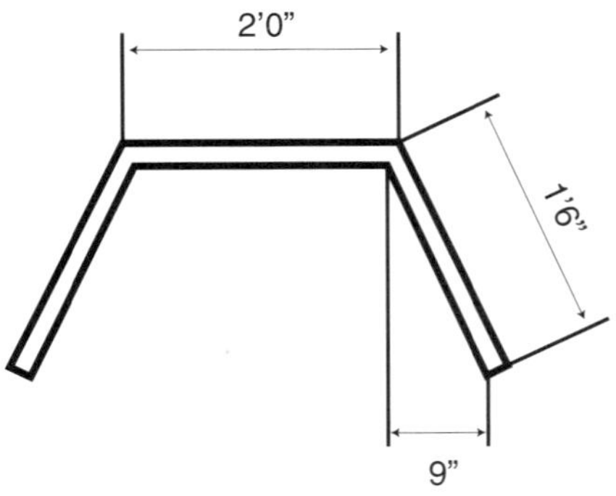

Why is the head of a person so often "cut off" when viewing a decorative mirror at a distance? This effect occurs because the mirror is often installed improperly with a long wire on the back and one nail in the center, causing the mirror to tilt forward. The decorative mirror will remain more vertical if properly installed (see Appendix).

Check the bottom of mirrors. In a situation where a dressing mirror is needed, such as on the inside of a closet door, the bottom of the mirror for that same 6'2" man can be approximately two feet off the floor for him to see his whole body in the mirror. This can produce a cost savings, especially for a builder doing multiple houses. Although some may want the aesthetic appeal of a mirror going from the floor to the top of the door, for instance, that mirror will reflect a lot of carpet in the foreground (see Figure 2.3).

Figure 2.2 *Our heads are one-half normal size when measured in the mirror from a distance of 1'6". This means, unless aesthetic considerations are involved, a 6'0" high mirror will suffice in most situations.*

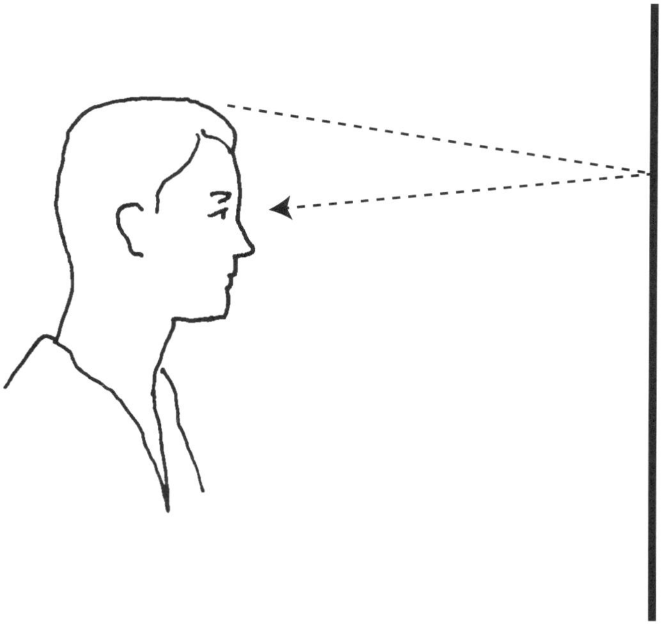

Figure 2.3 *The law of reflection showing the bottom of a 6'2" man's feet reflected in the mirror.*

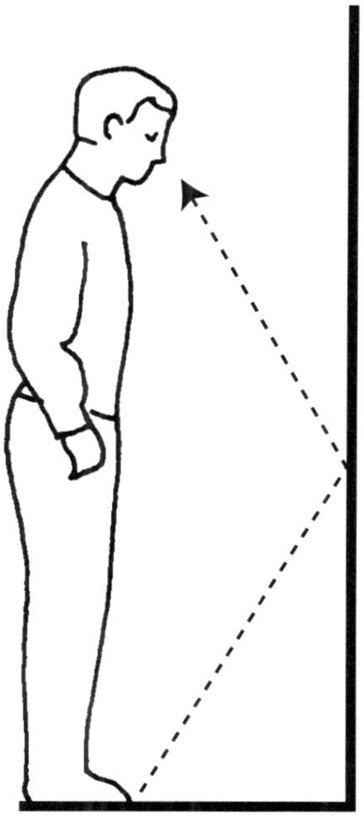

Private Realms

A series of bathrooms

A dramatic bathroom in Florida has cast stone columns and arches flanking a trompe l'oeil painting of the gardens of Versailles and mirror. The painting is duplicated in the mirror. The home, at Admiral's Cove, Jupiter, Florida, won the 1994 Aurora Award as best custom home. Jim Karmas, the designer and builder, said, "Two keys for upscale homes are the powder room and master bath. They have to be dramatic and appealing" (see Plate 7).

Galaxy Glass, in Pine Brook, New Jersey, has two vignette sample powder rooms to give high-end clients and designers ideas for unusual mirror techniques (see Plate 8).

Thomas Pheasant's glamorous ladies' bath, (see Plate 5), with its spot-lit flowers in crystal vases, antique mirror frame contrasted with the bronze mirror wall, and floral tapestry wall reflected in the distance, is less a spot for grooming than for restful repose and contemplation. With a totally different attitude, however, he has designed two bright, minimalist high-tech bathrooms.

The master bathroom by Thomas Pheasant features a round mirror suspended in front of a glass block wall. The mirror can be tilted. In the daytime, in particular, the lighting is excellent for grooming: it is bright and diffuse. Supplies are neatly stored in the curving cabinet doors and drawers to the side (see Plate 9). Another bathroom designed by Thomas Pheasant also features abundant natural lighting and an interplay of textured glass with mirror (see Plate 10).

An attractive solution is the bathroom by Kathleen Donohue of Portland, Oregon. She installed rose-colored marble on the walls of a bathroom and placed sconces with shades alongside the decorative mirrors. The reflections from the warm colored marble and the shades impart a pleasant light. She also designed ample shelves and custom paneled cabinetry (see Figure 2.4).

Multiple reflections

Sam Botero placed mirror on the cabinet doors of an elegant beige marble bathroom. The large globe lights are reflected in the multiple mirrors (see Figure 2.5).

In a dramatic touch, Clare Fraser had the ceiling of a long, narrow bath painted glossy black. The multiple mirrors reflect it and the contrasting white ceiling trim. The horizontal black-and-white tile wainscoting helps unify the many reflections in the room. In addition, the wainscot blocks certain reflections, such as those in the toilet area (see Figure 2.6).

The bathroom by Bebe Winkler has a large platform tub with many mirrors on the ceiling and around the dressing area (see Figure 2.7).

WHIMSEY

Bathrooms can also have a sense of fun. Liza Lerner took an old-fashioned kitchen sink and dressed it up with brass fittings. The light over the antique mirror is a traditional picture light. One's reflected face thus becomes almost a portrait on the wall (see Figure 2.8).

Figure 2.4 *Design: Kathleen Donohue, Neil Kelly Designers/Remodelers. Winner NKBA competition 1993. Photo: David Livingston. Courtesy of the National Kitchen & Bath Association.*

Other details

Sinks and grooming areas: One difficulty in grooming areas is that individuals need to lean over the sink when grooming themselves. One way to alleviate this is to have a sink or vanity with variable widths, or an angled vanity.

Mirrored shower doors: Mirrored shower doors are popular, with the mirror being on the

Figure 2.5 *A small bathroom. The lights are amplified by the mirrors and the light colors in the space. Design: Samuel Botero Associates, Inc. Photo: Phillip Ennis.*

room side rather than on the shower side. The doors must be protected with special tapes designed to prevent the shattering of the mirror if someone were to fall against it. The tapes look like laminated plastic when viewed from the shower side. Another approach would be to use tempered pyrolytic mirror, which will not deteriorate in moist conditions.

Figure 2.6 *Black-and-white bath with mirrored walls. Design: Clare Fraser. Photo: Derrick & Love.*

Figure 2.7 *Glamorous mirrors, ceiling, and walls reflect a collection of bronze sculpture. The bath also includes a satin chaise longue, onyx tub surround, and mirrored vanity table. Design: Bebe Winkler, Bebe Winkler Interior Design. Photo: Schild/Obremski.*

MIRRORS AND MOISTURE

Water is the enemy of silver-backed mirror. The material must be installed carefully to prevent the entrapment of water at the bottom of the mirror. This is particularly important in water- and steam-filled bathrooms. An unattractive result of trapped water is a deterioration of the silver backing, resulting in "black edge." An embassy in Washington has this condition in a public ladies' room; a beautiful vase of flowers in front of it does not conceal the condition (see Appendix).

Figure 2.8 *Bath in a remodeled and restored Vermont farmhouse. Design: Liza Lerner. Photo: Marcus Devoe.*

Silver-backed mirror is not recommended for the walls in shower areas, since the direct contact with water can result in damage to the silver. However, special anti-fogging shaving mirrors have been developed so that men can shave in the shower. An anti-fogging mirror has a valve behind it for the insertion of hot water so that the mirror is the same temperature as the surrounding air; hence, water will not condense on it. These mirrors

Figure 2.9 *Fog-free mirror from Mystic Mirror. Courtesy of Mystic Mirror and the Four Seasons Hotel, Washington, DC. Photo: Maxwell MacKenzie.*

are easily installed by do-it-yourselfers. Similarly, hot water pipes have been run behind mirrors in vanity areas to prevent fogging, or condensation, and the Mystic Mirror uses electric wiring to produce the same effect (see Figure 2.9).

A RESTROOM IN A MEDICAL OFFICE

Alison LeVino-Jones gave a restroom in an office a subtle contact with the outdoors. The large mirror was suspended over the window with a Plexiglas frame, thereby continuing the glass wall into the window, and providing extra lighting on the occupant's face (see Figure 2.10).

Figure 2.10 *Doctor's office suite. Design: LeVino-Jones Medical Interiors, Inc., Atlanta. Photo: Michael Turner.*

Dressing areas

Grooming does not have to occur primarily in the bathroom. A more gracious approach was created by Noel Jeffrey for a Kips Bay show house with a skirted table and antique accoutrements (see Plate 11).

Most residences do not have room for triple mirrors, but there are simple ways of incorporating them into the interior. Tom Welch, a Chicago architect, is remodeling an old building using mirrored closet doors. With a central mirror panel and two doors hinged adjacent to that panel, the triple mirror is easily created (see Figure 2.11).

The folding mirrored screen is another available approach. These screens provide privacy, brighten corners, and can be adjusted to permit views of the sides of the individual. A variety of styles are available, and they can easily be custom designed.

Builders in the Houston area have begun expanding the size of their closets to incorporate dressing areas with built-in cabinetry and mirrors. These are usually placed contiguous to the bathrooms.

Another popular location for mirrors, especially in bedrooms that are smaller, or that do not have walk-in closets, are sliding doors. A number of prefabricated units are on the market. In America these are often 6'8" high. However, in Europe they are often the height of the ceiling.

Figure 2.11 *Triple mirror created with standard mirrored closet doors.*

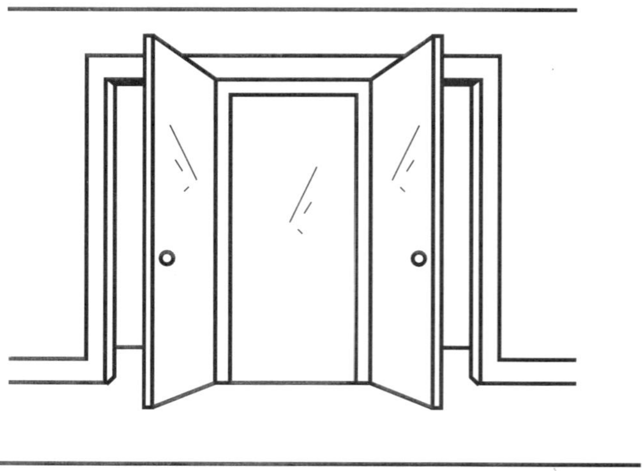

Bedrooms

The decorative mirror can be a dramatic accent in the bedroom. Ron Bricke contrasted a white framed mirror with a black wall and a lavish draped bed (see Plate 12). Frankie Welch placed an antique mirror atop curtaining over a bed area. The mirror picks up elements of the pillows and curtains (see Figure 2.12).

Figure 2.12 *Alexandria bedroom. Design: Frankie Welch. Photo: Vincent Ricardel.*

Larger panels of mirror can be built in adjacent to the bed. California designer Carole Eichen inset a mirror behind the bed, then rimmed it with shelving (see Figure 2.13).

A Washington bedroom/grooming area had movable mirrors (without a medicine cabinet behind them), shelving behind the bulletin board, a flip-up top on the counter for storage of cosmetics and creams, and storage columns behind the bed. The author's first private job, it was an early experiment in using mirrors spatially, and in eliminating clutter (see Figure 2.14).

Figure 2.13 *Vista Valle master bedroom.*
Design: Carole Eichen, Carole Eichen Interiors, Inc.
Photo: Jeffrey Aaron.

ENVIRONMENTAL LOADING

Environmental psychologists have developed a system to compare diverse environments, based on the amount of information perceived in the environment in a given amount of time, or the amount of stimuli processed by the observer. A term used by Albert Mehrabian is *load*. A predictable, neutral environment is low-load. An environment containing surprise, complexity, and variety is high-load. Mehrabian goes on to say, "Bedrooms used

Figure 2.14 *Berenson bedroom, 1970. An early experiment in clutter control in a sleeping/grooming area. Design: Pamela Heyne. Photo: Paul Segal.*

primarily for sleeping do not have to be loaded, but they should be pleasant.... A bedroom which will also be a prime sexual locus should probably contain more load. One of the reasons waterbeds are popular in motels which are known to be trysting places is that the rocking and somewhat unpredictable motions of such beds serve to increase arousal. There should be a source of music in a bedroom; colored lights might also be considered" (Mehrabian, p. 93). These, along with television movies, could provide a "desired increase in arousal level." While Mehrabian does not specifically mention mirrors, mirrors have long played a role in environments oriented to amorous pursuits.

"Honeymoon suites" in hotels and motels often have mirrored ceilings as well as mirrored panels near the bed, and abundant mirrors in the bathing areas. The bath, sunken and large enough for two, is occasionally removed from the bathroom altogether and placed in the bedroom. The goal of the designers typically has been to make the environments as stimulating and novel as possible.

An exercise room

Many exercise rooms are based on the traditional dance studio, with a wall of mirror on at least one long wall. Ever since the days of Degas, dancers have needed to see their reflections in the mirror to help them learn routines and to check their movements against those of their instructors. Safety mirrors are recommended in these areas.

In public and in private exercise rooms, television is an important component. When exercise equipment is sold on television, an oft-heard comment is, "You can do it while watching television." People like to allay the boredom of doing exercise by looking at television, and, in the home environment, they often use exercise tapes. However, television sets are not always things of beauty, particularly when reflected in a mirror.

Harcodium Design in Washington, DC, hid the television set behind a transparent mirror. When the set is turned off, the mirror looks like any other mirror (see Figures 2.15 and 2.16).

The Public Realm

In the public realm, overlapping uses of the mirror are more common. The mirrors at Versailles not only amplified space and light, but also permitted elaborately dressed and coifed courtiers to catch glimpses of themselves and others.

During the 19th century in the public realm, the restaurant became an important institution, often with mirrored panels. Opera houses, theaters with their mirrored foyers, department stores with mirrored columns, and fairs with mirror exhibits permitted everyone to enjoy the delights of reflections. People were also able to check on their appearance with greater regularity.

In the home, the hall stand was an important element in an area where little furniture existed. It usually contained hooks for coats and hats, typically a marble ledge, and a mirror. It helped visitors to the home assess who was in, depending on the clothes present. Today we have far more possessions, and we keep coats and hats in closets as much as possible. Most residential foyers have some sort of mirror as an aid for those passing through (see Plate 13).

Resort hotels and restaurants are often designed to cater to the guest's desire to make a grand entrance, and to check appearances before making that entrance. Invariably, mirrors are placed near the entrance.

Elevator lobbies are also important locations for mirror. Mirrors can allay the boredom of waiting for elevators. When installed in elevator lobbies, people stop complaining about slow elevators. People can rarely avoid looking at themselves. Mirrors in elevator lobbies can also be a safety factor, helping those in the elevator see any suspicious-looking individuals.

Mirrors also help patrons feel less isolated in restaurants. Pearl's, a New York restaurant designed by Gwathmey-Siegel, was 14 feet wide and 100 feet long The architects installed mirror on the upper reaches of the long side in order to make the space look wider. The owner later requested that mirror also be installed at the far end of the space, so that patrons sitting there would feel more a part of the front of the restaurant.

Another New York restaurant, Ruskay's, used a simple device of dark-colored walls, semicircular mirrors, and tall white candles to transform its fast-food decor into a more soothing and mysterious atmosphere. Even the counter had tall white candles on it, which made the lone diner seem not like a subject in an Edward Hopper painting, but a participant in a more festive environment (see Figure 2.17).

The Barista Brava coffee shop chain has used cheerful colors, and mirrors at a slight tilt to emphasize the activity, rather than the space, in the small shops (see Plate 14). The tilted mirror has a long tradition of use, particularly in restaurants in Latin countries.

Another important use of mirrors in the public realm is seeing how clothing looks prior to purchase. The I. Miller Shoe Salon uses abundant mirror, both as a means of expanding space and a way to help the potential purchaser become an actual purchaser.

Figure 2.15 *An exercise room with transparent mirror.*
Design: Harcodium Design. Photo: Dan Harris.

Figure 2.16 Television set shines through the transparent mirror. Design: Harcodium Design. Photo: Dan Harris.

Spur walls have fluorescent lighting behind them to provide even, yet soft, illumination for the customer (see Figure 2.18).

Sometimes shoe salons use tilted mirrors on the floor. A difficulty with them, however, is that they do not show the customer's entire form.

***Figure 2.17** Ruskay's restaurant, New York, 1973.*
Design: Carl Laanes. Courtesy of Today's Architectural Mirror.

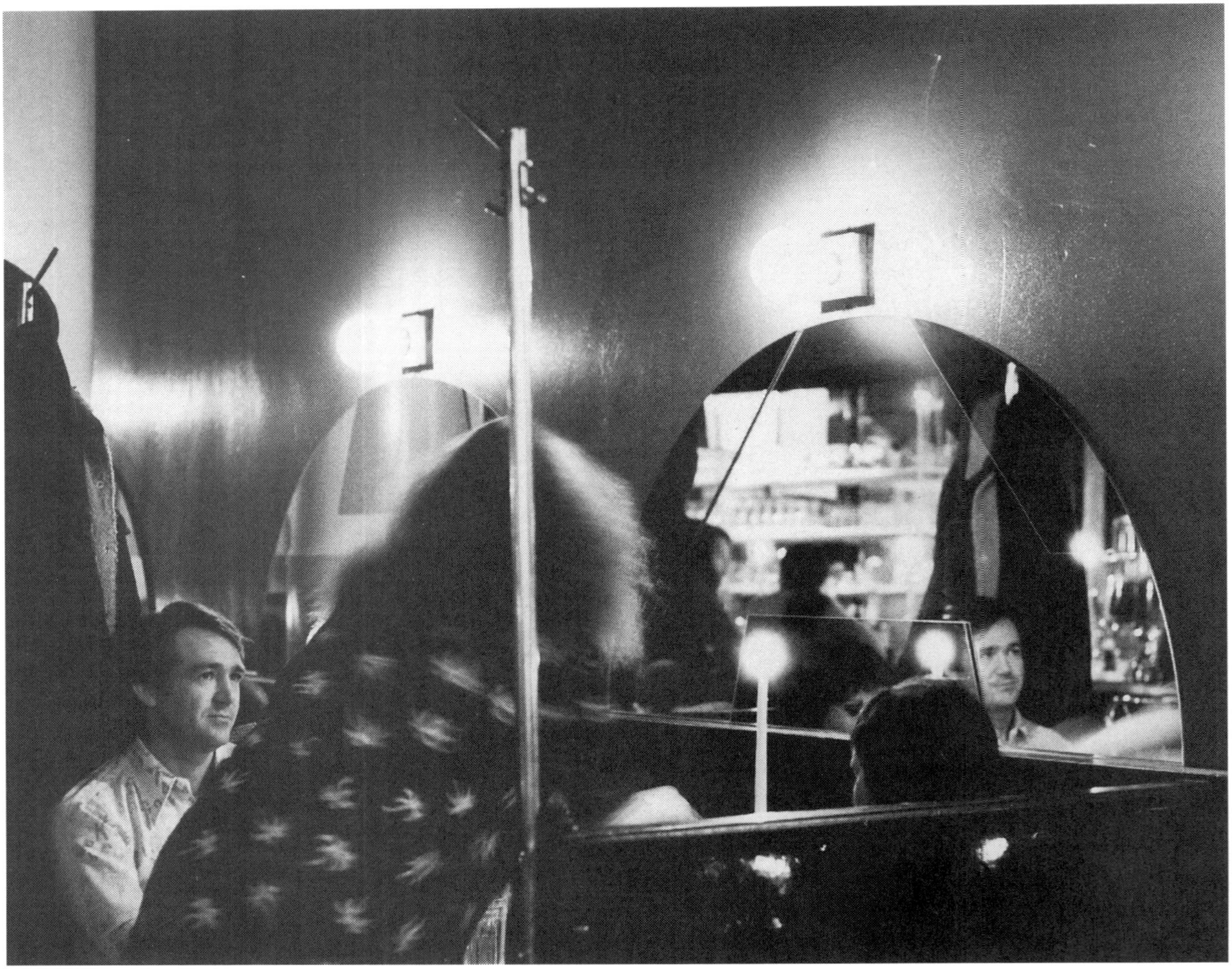

Figure 2.18 *I. Miller Shoe Salon, New York, 1962. Design: Victor Lundy. Photo: George Cserna. Courtesy of* Today's Architectural Mirror.

Specialized Uses

Psychological aspects

Mirrors play an important role in psychological treatment. For people with low self-esteem, mirror work might include looking at the body in the mirror for brief periods during the day. For people with missing limbs, a problem called "phantom limb" exists, in which the person "feels" the pain in the missing body part. By using a mirrored device, the brain can be tricked into thinking that the missing limb exists; hence, the pain experienced when the limb was severed can be eradicated.

As they age, people often say, "I just don't recognize myself in the mirror anymore." As our faces change with age, our perceptions also have to change. However, psychiatrists have noted that individuals with Alzheimer's disease simply do not recognize themselves in the mirror. They think the image in the mirror is not of themselves, but, rather, of some "stranger." One elderly woman with Alzheimer's disease refused to take a bath, thus causing herself physical and social problems. Eventually, therapists discovered that she was nervous about the stranger in the mirror who was watching her take a bath. The stranger, of course, was herself. When the mirror was painted over, she had no difficulty bathing.

For certain mentally ill patients, mirrors are a source of suspicion. They feel someone is "behind" the reflection. In certain instances they are correct, because transparent mirrors have often been used in mental hospitals.

Not all associations with mirrors are negative for the mentally ill. A National Institute of Mental Health representative reported an increased interest in personal appearance among some patients when mirrors were present. Additionally, patients preferred seeing mirrors with a rounded top, as opposed to mirrors with a squared-off top.

The true mirror

Developed by physicist John Walter, the true mirror eliminates the "mirror image" or reverse image. The mirror consists of two mirrors placed at a right angle. The joint is minimized since first-surface mirrors are used, with the reflecting plane at the top surface, rather than standard mirrors, with the reflecting plane behind the glass. These mirrors have had tremendous popularity from individuals who want to know what they really look like. Those in image-related fields have been avid customers. However, there are some drawbacks. Applying makeup or shaving with them is difficult, since most people have been conditioned by regular mirrors. In addition, true mirrors take up more space in the room than regular mirrors, since the mirrors extend out from the wall at a 45-degree angle.

Mirrors for the physically challenged

People in wheelchairs require sinks that permit the wheelchairs to slide under them. Additionally, they need mirrors over those sinks that are tilted forward to reflect their faces with ease.

Concave mirrors

These are readily available in mirror shops and bath shops. Typically, they are mounted on the wall or a stand and are adjustable.

Convex and dome mirrors

These are glass or plastic mirrors designed to prevent accidents in corridors, to assist motorists, to prevent theft in stores, to assist choirmasters, and to keep tabs on children in day care centers. The convex mirror appears flatter, while the dome mirror has a more decidedly spherical shape.

A 360-degree dome is used in four-way intersections and in shops. It was also recently used in a day care center over a baby-changing area to permit the attendant to observe other children in the space while she was busy (see Figure 2.19).

A 180-degree dome is used for two-way intersections.

A 90-degree dome or quarter dome is used for two-way L intersections.

Mirrors for infants and toddlers

Day care centers also make extensive use of plastic mirrors as devices to assist with child development. They are used in conjunction with inclined planes as a lure, in chin-up areas, on trays, in exploration corners, and in playpens and combined with soft large blocks. Babies love looking at themselves in the mirror; even though the plastic mirrors are not as optically perfect as glass mirrors, this is not a problem with small children. Their light weight and unbreakable quality are important considerations.

Figure 2.19 *Child care center with a dome mirror over the baby-changing area and a plastic plane mirror next to the pad. Photo courtesy of Jeanne Comeau.*

Transparent mirrors

Harcodium Design incorporated transparent mirror into a Washington area exercise room. These mirrors are also used as surveillance windows in stores, in police station lineups, and in gambling casinos.

A commonly used transparent mirror is Mirropane E.P., manufactured by Libbey-Owens-Ford. The product is ¼ inch gray tint glass with a chemical vapor deposition process on the front of the glass with 60 percent reflectance and 12 percent transmittance of light. It is intended for interior use. In a brightly lighted room it looks like any ordinary mirror. This is called the subject side. In a dimly lighted room it looks like a tinted glass window and is transparent. This is called the observer side.

Orientation: The reflective surface must face the brightly lit subject side.

Lighting: Subject-side lighting should be evenly distributed and should not shine into the mirror. Observer-side lighting should be dim with no high-intensity light sources visible. The ratio between subject-side and observer-side lighting should be ten to one.

Colors: Subject-side should be bright and uniform, and observer-side should be subdued, nonreflective, and uniform with no contrasting colors.

To minimize read-through: It is important to keep people and objects as far away as possible from the glass. Pinpoints of light, such as flashlights or cigarettes should be avoided.

At a Washington, DC, area restaurant, the transparent mirror is an interesting device to allow parents to keep an eye on their children while the parents are having a quiet, candlelit dinner. The parents and children are separated by a transparent mirror. The children are in a kids' realm, brightly lighted. The parents are in a quieter, more dimly lighted region. The parents see the children through the mirror, while the children are blissfully unaware that their table manners are being observed.

3

Mirrored Accents

"*Mirror is mysterious.* In large shimmering sheets, it can change the shape and size of a room. In small flashes, it can catch the sparkle of light the way a jewel catches the sun. Mirror is by nature glamorous and gay." (Baldwin, p. 115)

Like the pool in the garden, the mirrored accent adds sparkle and vitality to its setting. The framed mirror might brighten a dark corner. Not to be overlooked are the myriad of mirrored screens, place mats, and table tops or various tinted, patterned, or textured mirrors. Small segments of mirror can become "jewels," as Baldwin said; examples of this exist in the work of John Soane, in Indian Mogul tiles, and in Iranian cut mirrorwork. Particularly in the Iranian mirror work, the mirror is the essence of scintillation.

Another way to use the mirrored accent is according to the Chinese philosophy of feng shui, the art of placement. Mirrored accents are used to improve the yin and yang of dwellings and places of work.

Framed Mirrors

There are many venues for the mirrored accent. Perhaps the most common is the framed wall mirror.

As mirrors began to be made of glass rather than metal, frames were needed to protect the edges of the glass, and to add to their decorative or allegorical character.

Old mirrors are more commonly available today than one would think. Chairs and other pieces of furniture received daily wear and tear; hence, they did not always survive. Mirrors, however, particularly those in the great houses of Europe, tended to remain in one spot on the wall, and were often passed down from generation to generation (see Figure 3.1).

Another remnant from the past is the pattern book, a source of inspiration for current manufacturers of mirror frames, whether in carved wood or various composition materials.

Today, the framed mirror is often used as a stylistic accent. A Hepplewhite style or Regency style mirror may be juxtaposed with modern comfortable furniture. A great advantage of the framed mirror in our modern peripatetic society is that we can take it with us.

The framed mirror that we know today is a result of improvements in glassmaking that date from the end of the 17th century. Also, many of the styles of frames created then and during the next centuries are still with us today. (See Figures 3.2 and 3.3.)

"Whereas sixteenth and early seventeenth century Italian furniture had influenced the rest of Europe, late seventeenth century Italian furniture began in turn to be influenced by the French."(Child, p. 257) Mirrors, and mirror frames, reflected the rapidly changing tastes of society in France, as well as a high level of artistry and craftsmanship. At the end of the 17th century, many framed mirrors conveyed the formality and grandeur of Louis XIV, the Sun King. Although derived from Italian baroque (see Figure 3.2), its effect is more controlled. The rectilinear shaped frame, six feet wide, has a separate, ornate cresting flanked by two serious-looking putti (see Figure 3.4). This type of frame would typically have been used in a room with uncomfortable, straight-backed upholstered chairs and perhaps an impressive chest by Boulle, the ebeniste in the French court, skilled in brass and tortoiseshell inlay.

The successor to Louis XIV was his young grandson, Louis XV. Since he was too young to be king, a regent, Phillippe d'Orleans, was appointed to serve in his place from 1715 to 1723, giving the name "Regency" to the period. This is a transitional style between the baroque and rococo periods. It is typified by the beginnings of curved forms in wall panels and increased attention to smaller-scale, comfortable furniture.

A Regency giltwood mirror typifies this transitional style with etched figures and love emblems on the rectilinear border (see Figure 3.5). The upper cresting now contains mirror. A slightly later giltwood mirror (Figure 3.6) demonstrates the full-blown Louis XV rococo style with curving top and glass inserts covered with leaves and vines.

By this time, the aristocracy had fled the stifling monotony of Versailles and created

Figure 3.1 *Irish George III giltwood mirror. Courtesy of Christie's Images.*

Figure 3.3 *An Italian lead-framed mirror, early 18th century. Courtesy of Christie's Images.*

Figure 3.2 *Italian giltwood mirror, 17th century. Courtesy of Christie's Images.*

Figure 3.4 *Louis XIV giltwood mirror with convex-molded frame carved with foliage and berried vines. Courtesy of Christie's Images.*

Figure 3.5 *A Regency giltwood pier glass. Courtesy of Christie's Images.*

Figure 3.6 *A Louis XV rococo style giltwood mirror. Courtesy of Christie's Images.*

more intimate environments for themselves in chateaux and Parisian townhouses and apartments. Comfortable furniture, such as the chaise longue, and numerous small and convenient tables abounded. The role of women was more evident, with certain chairs designed to accommodate women's voluminous dresses. The bergère, with its low armrests, was typical. Dressing tables came into being, such as the *table à coiffer,* which had a movable mirrored top. The boudoir (deriving from the French "bouder," meaning to pout) also became an important room.

With the discovery of the ruins of Herculaneum and Pompei in 1748, a new interest in the classical world ensued, which influenced architecture and interiors. While furniture still had a comfortable appearance and small scale, curving legs and scrollwork were replaced by more severe classical forms and fluting. Chair and table legs looked like small tapered classical columns. Marie Antoinette loved to escape from the formality of court life at Versailles to smaller apartments at Versailles, the Petit Trianon, and Fontainebleau. And, rather than embodying earlier grandeur, some motifs were of classically clad maidens and graceful urns, as well as garden tools and musical instruments, motifs particularly relevant to Marie Antoinette.

Two excellent examples of pier mirrors in the new French style reside in Monticello, Thomas Jefferson's hilltop home in Virginia. Although most Americans of that era generally imported English mirrors, Jefferson had served as ambassador to France, and had developed a taste for French wines and some of the French decorative arts. The mirrors were installed in the parlour at Monticello, flanking the double doors (see Figure 3.7). They were made of two plates of glass in the center, surrounded by a border of smaller rectangular mirrors with joints concealed by molding.

After the fall of the monarchy in France, the Directoire style arose from 1795 to 1799, evincing a simplicity and delicacy, based on Roman republicanism. With the ascent of Napoleon in 1799 as consul, tastes became more exotic, incorporating Egyptian and animate forms as motifs. Crowning himself emperor of the French, King of Italy, and in control of most of Europe by 1807, Napoleon's power was emphasized by a simplified classicism based on Imperial Rome.

An important mirror developed at this time was called the "cheval" mirror by the English and "psyche" by the French. An adjustable dressing mirror, it was typically made of burr elm or ormolu-mounted mahogany with little surface ornamentation. Empress Josephine used this type of mirror at Malmaison.

After Napoleon's demise, the 19th century closed with great interest in French taste in England and America. Revivals of Louis XV and Louis XVI styles now symbolized elegance for the newly rich.

Figure 3.7 *Pier mirror in the parlor at Monticello.*
Monticello/Thomas Jefferson Memorial Foundation, Inc.
Photo: Edward Owen.

England

England lagged behind Italy and France in the production of glass and mirrors; hence, at the beginning of the 17th century, mirrors were rare and costly, and had importance as a vanity element. The charming stumpwork mirrors, framed with padded embroidery, are an example of the value of mirrors to an individual aristocratic household. These delightful mirrors were embroidered by gentlewomen, some in their early teens as they prepared for marriage. They contained allegorical allusions, symbols of piety, or personal expressions of the maker. The restoration of the monarchy in 1660 was also a subject for the frame makers. The frames were fitted with wooden or tortoiseshell trim and hinged rear struts by professional craftsmen, and often contained a case for their protection (see Figure 3.8).

As mirror making improved at the end of the 17th century in England, a more elongated form appeared (see Figure 3.9). These were called *pier glasses*, or pier mirrors, and were designed to be hung between windows. The William and Mary frames were often arched and decorated at the top with a form called "cushion moulded." The bottoms were usually plain to enable them to rest on a chair rail. Similar, though simpler in form, is the "Queen Anne." This style retains great popularity today, since the proportions are appropriate for smaller-scaled modern residences (see Figure 3.10).

Georgian age—England and America

George I ascended the throne in 1714. A year later, Lord Burlington published *The Four Books of Architecture* by the Italian Renaissance architect Andrea Palladio. The 18th century was known as the Age of Reason; hence, Palladio's classicism would find a fertile ground. Burlington had hired a protégé, designer William Kent, to create grand, neoclassic statements. Soon, thousands of country houses in England were built and renovated to conform to the classic style. Mirror frames were similarly neoclassic in style, often gilded, with rectilinear shapes and broken pediments. With the reign of George II, commencing in 1727, plainer wooden frames, similar to the type exported to the colonies, became popular.

French stylistic influences penetrated England, despite animosity based on wars and from groups such as the Anti-Gallican Society. The French rococo style was adapted with great fervor in the middle of the 18th century. Important in publicizing the style was the designer and furniture maker Thomas Chippendale. He published *The Gentleman and Cabinet-maker's Director* in England in 1754. A large folio, the book was comprehensive in its scope,

Figure 3.8 *Charles II parcel gilt and walnut stumpwork mirror. Courtesy of Christie's Images.*

Figure 3.9 Queen Anne walnut and parcel-gilt mirror with shaped rectangular divided, beveled plate. Courtesy of Christie's Images.

Figure 3.10 *Queen Anne reproduction mirror in Kittredge living room. Design consultant: Pamela Heyne. Photo: Garrison Studio.*

showing new designs for every type of furniture and decorative accessory. It capitalized on the 18th century British aristocrat's love of the Grand Tour and showed fanciful versions of Chinese, Gothic, and French rococo designs. *The Director* enjoyed great success in England and America.

Thomas Chippendale published his influential design book when he was in his early thirties. He became so successful that, at one point, he had 150 people working for him. Ironically, he was so influential and so widely copied that often only through bills of sale can the authenticity of his own work be proved. Some feel that Chippendale brazenly incorporated other designers' work, such as that of Mathias Locke, as his own. Yet, upon reading Chippendale's *Director*, one finds his enthusiasm is infectious. He wrote of "pier-glas frames and other ornaments, which I hope will give satisfaction to those who have them made." The half-dozen or so plates in his folio showing frames are exuberantly fanciful creations, with flowers, leaves, and vines overlapping the mirror, fretwork, icicles, columns, and perhaps a Chinese figure. The composition is often surmounted by a phoenix, the symbol of death and resurrection (see Figure 3.11).

These fanciful frames, often carved out of American pine and gilded, were generally the work of English carvers (see Figure 3.12). However, a few American craftsmen were up to the task, such as James Reynolds, one of the most important craftsmen in Philadelphia.

Most so-called Chippendale mirrors sold in the American colonies were derived from George II designs. No example of these designs exists in the Chippendale *Director.* Usually the frames were made of a mahogany veneer from the Caribbean, backed with a less expensive wood (the backing is sometimes a clue as to whether the frame was made in America or imported). Mahogany was a popular wood because it was easy to work, did not harbor insects, and came in pleasing colorations (see Figure 3.13).

The discovery of Pompeii in 1748 had a significant influence in England as well as elsewhere in Europe. Classical tastes would once again surge, although, this time, the large scale of Palladio was surmounted by a new delicacy inspired by Pompeii. Robert Adam was a Scottish architect who trained in Italy in the 1850s, early in his career. The experience would have a lasting impact. Adam and his brother were among the most influential architects of their time, incorporating unified, delicate antique patterns into their interiors. While many Adam mirror designs were built-in, such as over mantels, numerous sketches for individual framed mirrors exist.

A typical Adam mirror frame design might be rectilinear or oval, often with garlands and filigree at the bottom as well as the top of the frames, surmounted by an urn with flanking griffins. A summary of the Adams' work appeared in *The Works in Architecture,*

Figure 3.11 *Chippendale pier glass design from* The Gentleman and Cabinet-maker's Director, *1754. Courtesy of the Library of Congress, Rare Book Division.*

Figure 3.12 *Chippendale-style giltwood mirror with shaped divided plate flanked by columns. Courtesy of Christie's Images.*

Figure 3.13 *American Chippendale mirror, 1790. William Wilmerding of New York City—from Wunsch Americana Foundation. Courtesy of the New York State Museum, Albany.*

Figure 3.14 *George III giltwood mirror—crossed bough design. Courtesy of Christie's Images.*

which was published in 1773. A simplified Adam style mirror can be seen in Figure 3.14.

Whereas the Adams enjoyed great personal success in their time, two other important contributors to furniture design, George Hepplewhite and Thomas Sheraton, did not.

Little record of George Hepplewhite exists. It is presumed that he worked primarily as a designer, rather than a maker, of furniture in London from the 1760s until his death in 1786. His wife, Alice, continued the firm as A. Heppelwhite and Co., and two years later published a folio containing 300 Hepplewhite designs. Entitled *The Cabinet-maker*

Figure 3.15 *Pier glasses of Hepplewhite design, from* The Cabinet-Maker and Upholsterer's Guide, *1794. Courtesy of the Library of Congress, Microfilm Division.*

and Upholsterer's Guide, it gained great popularity in remote regions of England and America, popularizing neoclassic designs. Since the Hepplewhite firm was not located in a fashionable part of London, it was ignored by many there (Beard, p. 166). Hepplewhite frame designs were simpler than Adam frames. They were more vertical, tending to extend nearly to the tabletop. Alice Hepplewhite revised the folio twice, continuing to add to her husband's reputation (see Figure 3.15).

Thomas Sheraton published *The Cabinet-Maker and Upholsterer's Drawing Book* in 1791 and his *Cabinet Dictionary* in 1803. He favored simple, large-scale pieces, anticipating Regency designs, sometimes combined with dramatic festoons of drapery (see Figure 3.16). Yet, his lifestyle was far removed from the elegant designs he envisioned. Sheraton was described by a former employee:

> *He lived in an obscure street, his house half shop, half dwelling-house, and looked himself like a worn-out Methodist minister with a threadbare black coat...He had been a cabinet-maker, was now author and publisher, teaching drawing and I believe, occasional preacher. I was with him for about a week, engaged in most wretched work, writing a few articles and trying to put his shop in order, working among dirt and bugs for which I was remunerated with half a guinea. Miserable as the pay was, I was half ashamed to take it from the poor man.* (Child, p. 143)

Now, some two centuries later, Sheraton and Hepplewhite are household names.

The gilded mirror in the present-day Drysdale interior was derived from a Hepplewhite pattern book, with its carved drape and urn at the top of the frame. Mary Drysdale provided point and counterpoint, reflecting a classic bust in the mirror, and contrasting both with a minimalist-designed pier table (see Plate 15). In another view from the same modern apartment is a mirror derived from the early 19th century, the period of the British Regency. The frame shows intertwined sea serpents, alluding to the hegemony of the British navy over the seas and the prowess of Lord Nelson. The bold pillows are an appropriate counterbalance to the strong imagery of the mirror (see Plate 16).

The British Regency represented a simplified classicism. Furniture, as was the case in France, was often based on imperial Rome. A popular mirror during this period was the girandole mirror (see Figure 3.17) which was often embellished with sea serpents or eagles. The eagle occasionally had a ball and chain in its mouth. This motif derived from naval battles, wherein the opposing boat would be "demasted" when struck by flying cannonballs with their attached chains.

American Federal styles are similar to those of the British Regency period, albeit with references to American victories and ships.

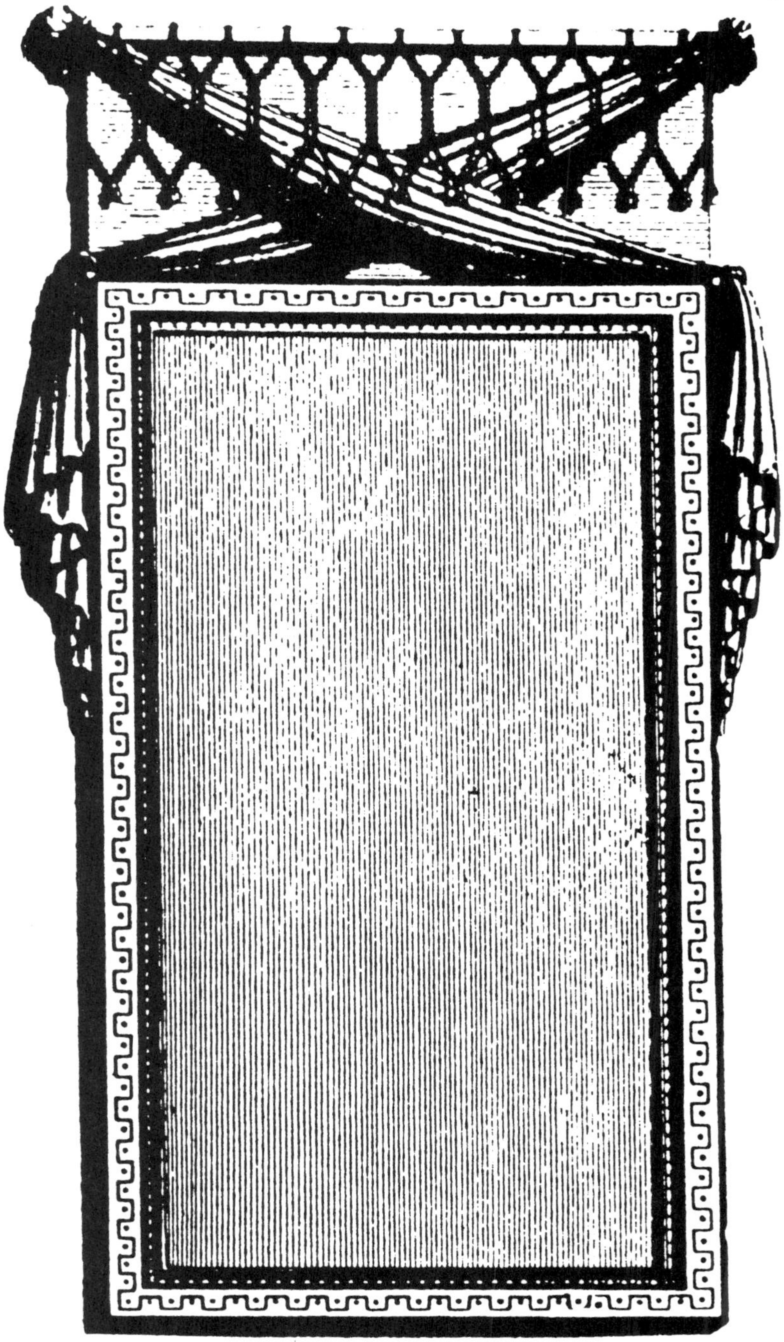

Figure 3.16 *Mirror frame design by Thomas Sheraton, British, early 19th century. From* The Furniture Designs of Thomas Sheraton. *Courtesy of the Library of Congress, Microfilm Division.*

Figure 3.17 *William IV giltwood convex mirror with circular plate within an ebonized border. Courtesy of Christie's Images.*

The Victorian era used overmantel mirrors and framed mirrors in a variety of decorative motifs, now often mass produced, for a mass market. Patronage of the aristocracy was now replaced by wealth of the middle classes.

Germany

The French rococo received particularly robust treatment in Germany. German woodcarving was virtuosic, as German symbols were incorporated. The German Biedermeier style was extremely popular from 1825 to 1860. Derived from French Empire forms, it assumed a solid and simple character. It was named for a newspaper character, "Papa Biedermeier," who represented bourgeois stability.

The twentieth century

In the 1920s and 1930s, the mirror was a popular decorative device. It was often used in formal ways, such as over a mantel, and was generally stripped of heavy frames.

Today we are in another gilded age, but the gilded framed mirror might just be resting against a wall (see Plate 17). Rather than having to be over a bureau or commode, it might have a quirky spot in a stairwell, one of Billy Baldwin's favorite touches. The framed mirror may even be found outdoors.

Many examples exist in this book of decorative mirrors floating over another wall mirror, probably tinted mirror. Today's mirror frame can be made of virtually anything. Decorative metal frames are popular today, as are reproduction frames and even old window sashes.

In the examples of interiors that follow, three common thoughts pervade the use of the framed mirror:

1. *Reflection.* What will be reflected from major points of view in the room?
2. *Scale.* Is the mirror intended to be a small object on the wall, or to make a major statement? A common problem is the too-small mirror that leaves a gap of a foot between the bottom of the frame and the top of the adjacent table or chest. This means that the lovely vase of flowers on the table does not get the reflection it deserves.
3. *Frame.* Is it appropriate? A narrow hallway may benefit from flatter frames in a mirror grouping, rather than deeper frames, which can obscure the mirror.

Billy Baldwin, the great 20th-century designer, loved using mirrors. He said,

> *Framed mirrors, of course, are beautiful anywhere. On the Left Bank in Paris, there is a white room 20 feet tall, with three immense windows curtained in red damask facing the Seine. Between them on each of the other walls hang five towering Louis Quinze mirrors. They are fantastically beautiful to look at, and they also serve, as mirrored walls would, to make the garden, trees, and river outside a living part of the room.* (Baldwin, p. 117)

Baldwin also preferred a mirror over a fireplace, feeling that a painting somehow competed with a fire. Over a sofa, he preferred built-in mirrors, as opposed to mirrors hanging on the wall. He disliked mirror over the bed and disliked mirrored furniture, but, as he said, "I do love to see little mirrored tables or stools with mirrored legs." He liked putting mirror on top of mirror, or putting an object, such as a "giant tortoiseshell smack in the middle" of a mirrored wall. He also loved the smallest of accents, saying,

> *Sometimes the greatest total effect you can get from mirror is to add up a lot of tiny slivers—octagonal flowerpots made of bands of mirror; embroidered pillows with little mirrors sewn in; fragments of mirror, like shining baguettes, on door panels, cornice moldings, and picture frames. As you walk past them the tiny quick twinkles of light catch the corner of your eye, giving the room a feeling of merriment and wit, and beautiful brilliance.* (Baldwin, p. 117)

Eclecticism

The comfortable second-story living room of Frankie Welch's 18th-century Alexandria townhouse is a skillful blend of old and new. The mirror over the mantel is an early 20th-century gilt-and-ebony piece. She has also placed a mirror on a cord between two windows (see Figure 3.18). Additionally, she has two built-in mirrors that tell an interesting story. Welch, noted for her corporate textile designs and fashion designs, had a chic women's dress shop on the first floor of the building for many years. One of her clients, a Washington celebrity, had not wanted to dress in a standard dressing room, so she asked to try on her clothes upstairs in private rooms. Welch installed the built-in mirrors for her. Years later, thinking them a bit plain, she had narrow gilt trim glued on top of the mirrors (see Figure 3.19).

Welch has juxtaposed her mirrors with rich warm colors and numerous festive, small-scale lighting sources. The distant chandelier contains shades over the fixtures and twisted fabric over the chain in a contrasting color.

Dining Environments

In a modern apartment of Ms. Welch's, she has used a lighter palette consisting of taupe and white with a few accents. The mirror in the dining room/library reflects the Venetian bust and was tilted sideways slightly to better reflect the bookcase (see Figure 3.20). The frame is actually made of some of Ms. Welch's textile designs, with red as the dominant color, providing a contrast with the white wall. Welch, once again, installed small shades

Figure 3.18 *An early-20th-century gilt-and-ebony mirror over the mantel and ornate framed mirror between the windows enhance the Welch living room. Design: Frankie Welch. Photo: Vincent Ricardel.*

Figure 3.19 Built-in mirror with gilt trim added for visual interest. Design: Frankie Welch. Photo: Vincent Ricardel.

over a chandelier; the reflection of that and the original border, based on textile designs, is reflected in the mirror.

In another dining area with light walls, New York designer Bebe Winkler has spotlighted floral accessories and used boldly colored chairs, juxtaposing modern with French 18th century elements. The black lampshade is itself an accent in the mirror and creates additional pools of light rather than uniform light (see Plate 18).

Some people do not like looking at themselves as they are dining. The Winkler/ Hallman dining room has a solution while still using mirror: a faceted mirror screen,

Figure 3.20 *Mirror with fabric frame reflects the dining table and bookcase. Design: Frankie Welch. Photo: Vincent Ricardel.*

carried up to the height of the molding. The chandelier, with its shaded fixtures, is multiplied in the faceted mirrors (see Plate 19).

In the Halvorson Rockwell design for the Jonathan Morr Espresso Bar, the mirror is tilted slightly forward to provide more views of the lively comings and goings in the coffee bar, rather than the ceiling (see Plate 20).

Small Mirrors

Small mirrors can be arranged in groupings and combined with paintings, such as in the Kittredge living room (see Figure 3.21). Or the mirrors can be integrated into panels or tile work, or used in traditional Iranian fashion to create shimmering geometric patterns. Architect Outerbridge Horsey, who admits to being influenced by the John Soane residence in London, used small insertions of mirror in an addition to a Washington residence (see Figures 3.22 and 3.23).

Mirrors have been important in India as small-scale shimmering elements on clothing, pillows, and other decorative accessories. They have long been used in conjunction with wall surfaces and tiles. The Amber Palace at Jaipur contains mirrors in small squares as part of a total decorative motif (see Figure 3.24). Other important uses of mirror in India are at the Red Forts in Delhi and Agra. A detail shows Shalimar tiles and decorative mirrors and tile (see Figure 3.25).

In Iran, mirrors have been used in palatial settings and shrines (see Plates 21 and 22). Among Iranian émigrés in Washington is Ghassem Mahjour, an artist skilled in cut mirrorwork, who previously worked on the Shah's palace. He imports mirrors, no thicker than a playing card, from Belgium. After creating a three-dimensional ground of plaster, he cuts and applies the delicate mirrors, resulting in dazzlingly complex designs. (His work is similar to that shown in Figure 3.26.)

Tinted Mirrors

Tinted mirrors are often used in large sheets, but can be used as smaller accents as well. The British Embassy in Washington, designed by Edward Lutyens, contains a ballroom with white walls into which are set panels of dark gray mirror. They form an elegant contrast to the white walls, and pick up the scheme of black-and-white marble flooring in the hallway.

Figure 3.21 *Grouping of small mirrors. Kittredge living room. Design consultant: Pamela Heyne. Photo: Garrison Studio.*

Figure 3.22 *View of the dayroom from dining room.*
Design: Outerbridge Horsey. Horsey and Thorpe Architects.
Photo: Charles Rumph.

Figure 3.23 *Breakfast room by Sir John Soane, English, early 19th century. Courtesy of the trustees of Sir John Soane's Museum, London.*

Figure 3.24 The Amber Palace in Jaipur, India. Courtesy of Air India Library.

Figure 3.25 *Shalimar tiles and decorative mirrors in the ceiling, Rajesthan, India. Photo: W. Swift Martin III.*

Figure 3.26 *The Persian room in the former Iranian embassy.*

Mirrored Furniture and Tabletops

Early mirrors associated with furniture often had a vanity function. By the 1920s and 1930s, designers began to sheath furniture with mirror. American designer Samuel Marx, for example, was an important innovator in Art Deco furniture, creating a coffee table covered with variegated mirror squares.

The amusing cabinet by Neotu, a New York store, designed by Elizabeth Garouste and Mattia Bonetti, consists of wood, leather, and mirrors in a free-form shape; are they clouds, or perhaps the spots of a cow (see Figure 3.27)? The same firm has created free-form light sconces combined with mirror.

Figure 3.27 *ATOLL cabinet. Designers: Elizabeth Garouste and Mattia Bonetti, 1994; manufactured by Neotu Paris and New York.*

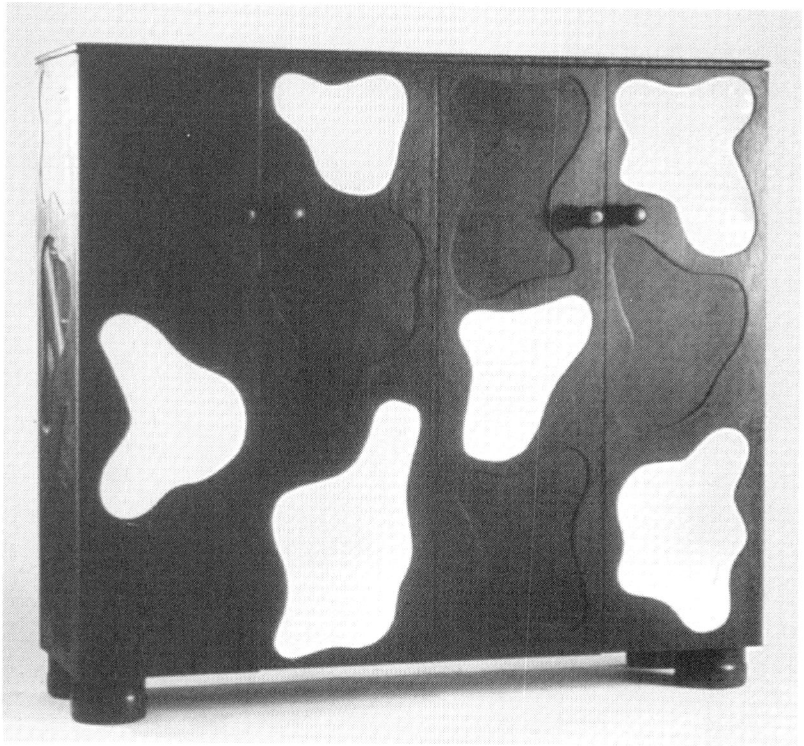

A number of products in the market today utilize mirror for sparkle. Headboards and shelving units are particularly popular. Many of the shelving units contain small-aperture built-in lighting. Mirrored cubes are useful and versatile as plant stands, or to display sculpture or pottery.

Mirror has long been associated with tabletops. In the 18th and 19th centuries, mirrored trays or plateaux would be located in the center of the dining room table. Simpler versions without the metal trim are still interesting centerpieces, as candles are reflected from below, and flowers reflected from diverse angles.

Mirrored place mats are extremely decorative. Their "glassiness" is enhanced if they are placed atop a dark tablecloth with a rough or sumptuous texture. The place mats are, of course, neutral accessories and pick up whatever seasonal decorative motif is present.

Mirrored Screens

Mirrored firescreens were developed in the 18th century because when fires were not blazing in the hearth, the space would look dark and grimy. These screens have elegant legs and decorative gold or ormolu trim.

Mirrored screens also have a distinct and versatile place in interiors, particularly in a dark room. Bebe Winkler used a mirrored screen in a dining area design (see Plate 19). The author made use of a faceted screen in her dining room as a cover for an electric panel box.

Thomas Pheasant created a custom wood-framed screen with mirror panels laminated with rippled glass placed in an alternating pattern in order to reflect light, rather than images (see Plate 23).

Feng Shui

Mirrors have been called the "Band-aid" of feng shui. Mirror is used in two distinct ways in feng shui: (1) in a symbolic fashion, to direct the flow of good and evil forces in one's environment and life, and (2) similar to Western approaches, as a means of ameliorating the building environment. For instance, a Chinese home might have a mirror on the outside of the house to protect the home from a variety of negative forces. Then, inside

Plate 1
Space, enhanced by mirror.
Design: Drysdale Design.
Photo: Andrew Lautman.

Plate 2 *View shifting. Portable view shifter conveys a view of the garden so that one does not have to look at the wall. Design: Pamela Heyne. Photo: Garrison Studio.*

Plate 3 *This sunlight at the bottom of a 100-foot-deep shaft is a direct result of a tracking mirror, or heliostat. Underground Space Center offices at the University of Minnesota. Design: BRW Architects. Photo: John Carmody. Courtesy of* Underground Space Design.

Plate 4 *Example of a carved design. Central mirror is reverse carved and inlaid with silver and gold leaf. Photo: Peter Rymwid. Courtesy of Galaxy Glass Corp. Inc.*

Plate 5 *Ladies' bath. A decorative mirror floats on a bronze mirror wall.*
Design: Thomas Pheasant Inc.
Photo: Maxwell MacKenzie.

Plate 6 *Hotel Beauharnais, Paris, early 19th century. Courtesy of the German Embassy, Paris.*

Plate 7 *Sylvan Estate Homes, Jupiter, Fla.*
Designer and builder: Jim Karmas.
Photo: Kim Sargent.
Courtesy of Luxury Homes *magazine.*

Plate 8 *Galaxy Showroom—The panels on either side of and above the mirror have been sandblasted to allow the introduction of lighting. A majority of the silver has been removed to form a pinstripe. Photo: Peter Rymwid. Courtesy of Galaxy Glass Corp, Inc.*

Plate 9 *Master bathroom with suspended mirror. Design: Thomas Pheasant, Inc. Photo: Ping Amarand.*

Plate 10 *A rippled glass window and frosted glass vanity create textural differences against the polished mirrored background. Design: Thomas Pheasant, Inc. Photo: Ping Amarand.*

Plate 11 *Dressing room for a Kips Bay show house. Design: Noel Jeffrey. Photo: Peter Vitale.*

Plate 12 *Ornate mirror in Kips Bay bedroom, 1994. Design: Ron Bricke & Associates, Inc. Photo: Michael L. Hill.*

Plate 13 *Entrance hall. Design: Gandy/Peace, Inc. Photo: Chris A. Little.*

Plate 14 *Barista Brava Coffee Shop. Design: Adamstein and Demetriou. Photo: Theodore Adamstein. Courtesy of Barista Brava.*

Plate 15 *Hepplewhite-style mirror in the Bradley/Rosenheim residence. Design: Drysdale Design. Photo: Mick Hales.*

Plate 16 *William II-style mirror in the Bradley/Rosenheim residence. Design: Drysdale Design. Photo: Mick Hales.*

Plate 17 *Leaning mirror in vignette for American Crafts Council in Atlanta. Design: Gandy/Peace, Inc. Photo: Chris A. Little*

Plate 18 *Small entry hall contains a dining table for four. The space is defined by an antique Irish giltwood mirror. Design: Bebe Winkler, Bebe Winkler Interior Design. Photo: Peter Margonelli.*

Plate 19 *Small living room and dining room combined; the dining area is defined by a five-paneled beveled mirrored screen. Design: Bebe Winkler, Bebe Winkler Interior Design.*

Plate 20 *Jonathan Morr Espresso Bar. Design: David Rockwell and Jay Haverson, formerly of Haverson/ Rockwell Architects. Photo: Paul Warchol.*

Plate 21 *Golestan Palace, Tehran. Magnificent example of mirrored ceiling which reflects decorative columns, cut mirrorwork, distant gardens, and throne. 19th century. Photo: Roloff Beny. Courtesy of the National Archives of Canada.*

Plate 22 *Tomb of Iman Reza, Iran. Photo: Roloff Beny Courtesy of the National Archives of Canada.*

Plate 23 *A wood-framed screen with mirror panels laminated with rippled glass to reflect light during the day and night. Design: Thomas Pheasant, Inc. Photo: Gordon Beall.*

Plate 24
Galerie des Glaces (Hall of Mirrors), Palace of Versailles, France, late 17th century. © Photo R.M.N.

Plate 25 Apartment of Louis XIV, Palace of Versailles, France, early 18th century. The new plate glass permitted larger amounts of mirror over fireplaces. © Photo R.M.N.

Plates 26 and 27
Waldorf Towers.
Design: Carleton Varney, Dorothy Draper & Co., Inc.
Photo: Peter Vitale.

Plate 28 Entrance hall. Mirror was used to amplify the space and to bring light from the opposite end of the apartment. Design: Thomas Pheasant, Inc. Photo: Maxwell MacKenzie.

Plate 29 Georgetown living room, finished design. Note use of lamp and ficus tree to block unattractive reflections in the distance. Design: Pamela Heyne. Photo: Garrison Studio.

Plate 31 City Cafe. A triangular space seems to be square because of the mirrored wall. Design: David M. Schwarz. Photo: Hedrich Blessing

Plate 30 *Kips Bay show house, New York. The mirror completes the form of the window. Design: Ron Bricke & Associates, Inc.. Photo: Michael L. Hill.*

Plate 32 *Clyde's Restaurant and Bar, Washington, DC. Design: Thomas Wright, Brown and Wright Architects. Photo: Seva Raskin*

Plate 33 *Kaleidoscope skylight.*
Design: Bruce Haney.
Photo: Bruce Haney.

Plate 34 *"Julia Child mirror" used to show tops of pottery to visitors at American Crafts Council.*
Design: Gandy/Peace, Inc.
Photo: Bard Wrisley.

Plate 35 *Angled mirror over fireplace.*
Design: Richar Interiors.
Photo: Heinrich Photography.

Plate 36 *Mills' view shifter window. Design: Pamela Heyne. Photo: William Mills.*

Plate 37 *Mills' view shifter window, exterior view. Design: Pamela Heyne. Photo: William Mills.*

Plate 38 *The completed periscope window. Design: Pamela Heyne. Photo: William Mills.*

the home, a mirror might be placed in the hallway to make the hall seem less narrow.

Feng shui originally derives from a Taoist reverence for nature. *Feng* means wind, *shui* means water. They are cosmic forces at the base of all existence. Two important concepts emanating from feng shui are "ch'i," a sort of cosmic breath, and "yin and yang," opposing forces of good and evil. Ch'i informs our personalities, the height of mountains, the color of flowers, the force of streams. Forces in nature and our personal lives must be in balance, and feng shui helps to achieve that balance. For the Chinese, the physical environment is directly related to a person's emotional sense of well-being and, hence, success in the outer world. If a home or office has good feng shui, the occupant's emotional life will be in balance, the person will feel happier and, thus, more productive, and will make more money. If a person, for instance, is working at a desk with his back facing the door, the person will feel tense and will be unproductive. The office has bad feng shui for him.

For international architect Alfred Liu, feng shui is simply based on common sense and designs that make the individual feel comfortable emotionally. He says, "Any building that looks good, feels good, and has good function...has good feng shui."

A road directed at the home is considered inauspicious, with "arrows" of evil influence directed at the door. The arrows would be "bad ch'i." Mirrors can be placed in ways to direct away the bad ch'i of the offending road. However, according to Alfred Liu, a road directed at certain structures—a state capitol or a cathedral, for example—is quite appropriate.

In the home, a screen and step would typically occur at the entrance to keep out evil forces. Mirrors are often placed in a window by occupants to reflect away the offending ch'i of neighboring buildings. For instance, angled buildings are considered hostile. I. M. Pei's Bank of China building, which is angular, seemingly is "cutting people." There have been reports of "mirror wars" in Hong Kong and Taipei, as mirrors in apartment buildings reflect and re-reflect off one another.

Feng shui also helps ameliorate architectural problems. If two doors are out of alignment, a mirror might be placed adjacent to one of the doors to dematerialize the wall. If a beam is oppressive in a room, a mirror might be placed there to lessen its negative qualities. And, in ways similar to those in the West, a mirror might be placed in a narrow hallway to make it seem less oppressive.

Intangible and tangible negatives are theoretically reflected by the mirror. The bedroom is an important location for mirrors. Mirrors are often placed so that one can see if an unwelcome individual is lurking at the door.

While some view feng shui as a philosophy geared to the superstitious, it has millions of adherents worldwide who are willing to pay considerable sums to have their environments analyzed by feng shui experts. Even Donald Trump has hired feng shui practitioners to ensure that projects using Chinese investors will appeal to their sensibilities.

Mary Lou Clark is an artist and feng shui advisor from Cohasset, Massachusetts. She feels feng shui has improved her environment as well as her financial and emotional life. She says, "Western thinking stresses rational solutions for problems. Nonrational, transcendental solutions may work better in certain instances" (see Figures 3.28 and 3.29).

Figure 3.28 *Mirror in kitchen over stove creates harmony in the kitchen according to feng shui. Design: Mary Lou Clark. Photo: Imants Ansbergs.*

Figure 3.29 *Mirror in bedroom illustrating feng shui design. This mirror relates to the well-being of a child. Design: Mary Lou Clark. Photo: Imants Ansbergs.*

4

Space

"Oh Kitty, how nice it would be if we could only get through into the Looking Glass House! I'm sure it's got oh! such beautiful things in it! Let's pretend there's a way of getting through into it, somehow, Kitty. Let's pretend the glass has got all soft like gauze, so that we can get through." (Lewis Carroll, *Through the Looking Glass*)

Most of us have, at one time or another, been fooled into thinking we can walk into the space a mirror conveys. Perhaps we saw it in a hallway, and, just like Alice, felt we could enter the illusions, until at the last minute we saw our own reflection.

From a design standpoint, sometimes we want to emphasize the illusionary qualities of the mirror. We simply want a room to look bigger, a ceiling to look taller. We are not interested so much in reflecting ourselves. We are more interested in space.

Of course, we know the decorative framed mirror can give a sense of space, but it always remains an objective plane. It does not disappear to the extent that the built-in mirror can. Nor will it seem to be a glass window into another realm, the way mirrored doors and windows with muntins can.

Illusion is a legitimate design goal. It can be achieved in four distinct ways with mirrors.

(1) *The built-in mirror:* Gilt trim, pilasters, paneling, and draperies all serve to make the mirror look like a void, opening into another realm. Today, we can select from

a series of traditional techniques or combine the mirror with drywall or brick arches, or bookshelves, closets, cabinetry, or latticework.

(2) *Illusionary glass doors and windows:* The mirror can look like clear glass on a door or window. Combined with muntins, people will have trouble telling the difference between the real glass doors and the mirrored doors. This is particularly useful where symmetry is desired.

(3) *Mirrored surfaces:* Mirror spanning an entire wall, or mirroring a ceiling, or even a portion of a floor, can be very illusionary. Occasionally, large sheets of mirror can be combined with columns or pilasters to give the illusion of a colonnade.

(4) *Subtle effects:* Tinted, antiqued, and beveled mirror can still convey a sense of space, albeit with less illusionism than clear mirror. These mirrors are popular where people "don't want to see themselves," or where the reflected view is not attractive.

Transformations

At Versailles, the mirror transformed the new corridor, designed to link the north and south apartments. Placed on the long side of the corridor, the mirrored arches duplicate the 17 arched windows (see Plate 24).

In our environments, we can create our own transformations, using techniques from the 17th century or from our own era. Particularly when using mirror spanning from wall to wall, no material transforms a space as quickly, as completely, or as inexpensively as mirror.

This dramatic ability of the mirror to transform a space instantaneously, one of its greatest advantages, also makes some people who use it rather nervous. If one remembers that mirror is simply a neutral material, however, and uses traditional or modern design techniques, the mirror can simply disappear from our consciousness. If properly used, it won't be "too much," for it simply will not "exist" from a perceptual standpoint.

The following is a list of general considerations that will affect how well we use this neutral material.

Law of reflection: What is likely to be reflected in the mirror? It is important to consider what is outside the window, even around the corner, as well as in the room. If negative reflections are likely, can they be masked with a lamp or a ficus tree, for instance?

Room dimension: Long, narrow rooms or corridors typically are enhanced by mirror on the long side. Corridors sometimes have mirrors at one end to reflect a far window as a way of brightening that area.

Mirrors and windows: Large sheets of mirror are usually placed perpendicular to or opposite windows; otherwise, the illusionary void of the mirror will compete with the real void of the windows.

Lighting: Chandeliers, sconces, and floor-mounted candelabra were important components at Versailles. Today, lamps with silk shades, pools of light, and pinpoints of light are more dramatic than evenly lighted interiors. A spotlight is most effective when lighting an object in the vicinity of the mirror, rather than the surface of the mirror itself. Spotlights focused on the mirror will result in reflections of the light and an emphasis of surface flaws, such as dust or streaks, on the mirror.

Color: The mirror will usually seem more illusionary if it is placed next to darker colors rather than stark white, which will emphasize the naturally greenish tinge of most mirrors. If white walls are to be used, the designer might consider ultra-clear mirror.

Mirrors and decorative items: Certain chests and tables can abut the mirror. However, beware of horizontal items. A horizontal tapestry, a horizontal bank of curtains, or a bed, placed perpendicular to a mirror will look twice as long. However, sometimes the designer may want to emphasize the horizontality of an element, such as a "floating" bench, by placing it perpendicular to a mirror.

Space, not clutter: A mirror is most effective if it reflects space. The cluttered living room or cluttered kitchen countertop will look more so in the mirror.

Multiple reflections: Mirrors at right angles will invariably convey views of the person entering the room. Whatever is in the corner will be reflected four times. Mirrors opposite one another convey ever-darker reflections in the distance. This effect can be mitigated with lights.

Seeing oneself: Remember Hugh Jacobsen's comment, "A mirror is a mirror when you can see yourself, otherwise it is an illusionary means of expanding space." The oblique mirror, the mirror above eye level, and the mirror in the far corner or under the kitchen cabinet all deemphasize the view of the individual. A painting placed on top of the mirror also deemphasizes the reflection of the person.

The Built-In Mirror

Mirrors at Versailles were not a last-minute addition, but were carefully considered, integral to the interior. They consisted of overmantel mirrors, pier mirrors, and faux doors, such as those in the Hall of Mirrors (see Plate 25).

The overmantel mirror

The overmantel mirror in the king's suite at Versailles is indicative of the ability of French craftsmen to create larger mirrors due to their development of plate glass. The overmantel mirror consists of only two pieces of glass. Also, it demonstrates the low-profile mantel, barely higher than the railing.

The overmantel mirror continues to be one of the most popular locations for mirror. Overmantel mirrors were traditionally placed opposite one another in grand ballrooms and rooms of state, such as the king's bedroom, which had a distinct ceremonial function, attended by courtiers who observed the king's rising, pronouncements, and retiring. This type of overmantel mirror set the standard throughout the 18th century, and continues to do so to this day (see Figure 4.1 and Plate 25).

Today, the vast majority of us have environments that are far less elaborate. In a modern apartment, dramatic color or lighting, such as the floor-mounted spotlight, will often have to suffice as we seek variety in the mirror's reflections.

Pier mirrors and mirrors in panels

Pier mirrors were initially designed to be installed on the often too-solid pier between glass doors and windows (see Figure 4.2). Mirrors were also set into panels along a wall and in panels above a door. Mirror set into a panel over a doorway can give the illusion of greater height to the door. Additionally, it takes up the gap between the window and the top of the door. Particularly in older houses, there is often a foot or more of space between the top of the door and the top of the window.

Figure 4.1 *Design of overmantel mirror by J. F. Blondel from his* De la distribution des maisons de plaisance, *1738. Courtesy of the Library of Congress, Rare Book Division.*

It is always desirable to paint the inside of the rabbeted trim (black is often recommended if the exterior is gold) so that unfinished wood will not be reflected by mirror. While it is possible to butt the trim to the glass, it is most effective if the trim overlaps the glass.

Mirrors set into panels along a wall might be in keeping with an older interior, particularly where the existing walls might not be flat and vertical.

Figure 4.2 *18th century illustration showing pier mirrors, a way of breaking up the massiveness of the piers between the glass doors and windows. J. F. Blondel,* De la distribution. *Courtesy of the Library of Congress, Rare Book Division.*

Draperies

Curtains can be another form of enframement. A stunning example exists in the bedroom of the Empress Josephine at the Chateau de Malmaison. A circular room contains curtains that, when juxtaposed with mirror, resemble an opening into another space (see Figure 4.3). At Malmaison, the illusion was intensified by concealing fastenings for the draperies, and concealing the end of the mirror at the top.

Figure 4.3 *Bedroom of Empress Josephine at the Chateau de Malmaison, France, 1810. The lavish curtains of the room act as frames for the mirrors, adding to their illusionary quality. © Photo R.M.N.*

Recent interpretations

The mirrors at Versailles are framed with bronze and marble pilasters and arches. While few of us can equal the elaborate materials, we can adapt the design ideas from Versailles to our environments today.

An overmantel mirror

A formal two-story living room contains a large overmantel mirror as an accent at the end of the room. The mirror is large enough to reflect the various architectural features and reflects the chandelier in the foreground. The mirror is an integral part of the overall architectural composition (see Figure 4.4).

An entrance hall

The entrance hall at the Waldorf Towers, by Carleton Varney, has painted wooden pilasters rimming the mirror, which, in turn, reflects the black-and-white diamond-pattern floor and the table set against the mirror. The walls are an intense cherry red, and furnishings are simple (see Plate 26).

A living room

A living room in the Waldorf Towers, also by Carleton Varney, features a tremendous cased opening with a mirror set into it. The addition of the yellow wood desk with spring flowers blocks the view of a person and emphasizes the space surrounding the furniture. As with the table above, this piece of furniture does not penetrate far into the room. The sense of space is emphasized (see Plate 27).

A media cabinet

Dealing with modern clutter is a challenge. Sometimes, 17th-century ideas can result in modern solutions.

A Washington businesswoman had a beautiful Georgetown living room, but needed an elegant way to store her audio equipment and CD collection. She already had a mirror flanking one wall of the fireplace. A second mirror was added to the other side of the fireplace, and two media cabinets were installed over the mirror. The CDs were stored in "columns" in front of the mirror. The speakers were installed in the "keystone," centered on the arch above the mirror, and audio equipment was stored in the "plinth," or base cabinet (see Figure 4.5).

Figure 4.4 *Two-story living room with a large panel of mirror above the fireplace to reflect back on the room. Photo: Peter Rymwid. Courtesy of Galaxy Glass.*

In this design, since the cabinetry was installed after the mirror, there is no problem in seeing the edge of the mirror. This results in a continuous view of lustrous wood in the mirror, rather than the dark edge of mirror. Also, the back of the cabinetry was finished the same as the front, to result in cleaner reflections.

If the mirror had been installed after this elaborate cabinetry, the installer would have had a difficult, though not impossible, job, cutting the mirror to conform to every indentation and curve.

We have seen how, at Versailles, the edge of the glass was always covered. And we have seen how, in turn-of-the-century magic tricks, the edge of the glass was also concealed—

Figure 4.5 *Georgetown media cabinet. The sense of depth is emphasized by the storage columns. Design of cabinetry: Pamela Heyne. Photo: William Mills.*

with a table leg, for instance. The edge of the glass had to be concealed for maximum illusion.

While it is desirable to conceal the edge of the glass, in many instances this is not possible. Inserting mirror into an existing niche or installing a wall of mirror with the edge of the glass butting the perpendicular corners are examples of such a situation. With proper measuring and close tolerances, however, the edge of the glass will not be noticed in these situations.

A KITCHEN

The backsplash area is a popular location for mirror. It reflects distant windows or the room's space, helps mothers keep an eye on their children while their backs are turned, and blends in with virtually any decor. Since this kitchen was for a speculative project in Georgetown, the neutral quality of the mirror was a desirable feature. Additionally, the spatial qualities were significant. As has been noted, the fact that the individual's reflection is partially concealed by the wall cabinets boosts the illusionism of this type of mirror (see Figure 4.6).

These mirrors are at a right angle. That means that items near the corner will be reflected four times, rather than simply one time, as would be the case with a single wall of mirror. This may be a problem if a client has a number of appliances that will be set on the countertop. Many commercial cabinet companies have appliance "garages" that cut down on the clutter.

A NEW YORK APARTMENT WITH DRYWALL "CUTOUTS"

Gamal El-Zoghby used mirror inserted into drywall circles and niches as a way of heightening the illusions of his designs. For him, mirror was a tool to dematerialize the walls and ceilings of the too-small New York apartment. He had to block out the walls and ceilings to create the geometric cutouts (see Figure 4.7).

MASONRY ARCHES AND LATTICE ARCHES

The brick arch combined with mirror can be quite illusionary. The chain restaurant, Mick's, in Washington, D.C., features a basement dining room. The room's deep brick niches contain mirror and handcrafted wooden toys or birds juxtaposed with the mirror. In a Washington garden, mirror was installed in brick arches. The mirror was installed on

Figure 4.6 *Georgetown kitchen for Richardson/Figge development project. Design: Pamela Heyne. Photo: Lisa Berg.*

Figure 4.7 *New York apartment with mirror inserted into the walls. Design: Gamal El-Zoghby, 1972. Photo: Robert Perron.*

a dark wall, and does not receive gleams of sunlight on the surface. It does reflect blue sky and plants, though. The reflection of the masonary surrounding the mirror adds to the sense of depth in the mirror (see Figure 4.8).

Figure 4.8 *Mirrored arch in a garden.*
Design: Kitti Von Kann. Photo: Pamela Heyne.

Illusionary Doors and Windows

As at Versailles, another way to expand the spatial feel of a room is to insert a glass "window" or "door." The mirror, particularly when combined with muntins to resemble French doors or windows, will seem to be "clear" glass, with a view of a distant room beyond.

The Hall of Mirrors gives the impression of looking through clear glass. The Salon of War at Versailles, leading into the Hall of Mirrors, has a similar mirrored treatment (see Figure 4.9).

The Salon of the Bull's Eye at Versailles has two oval windows mounted in the coved ceiling. One of the windows is real and admits the view of sky and sun. The second

Figure 4.9 *Salon of War, Palace of Versailles, France, late 17th century. © Photo R.M.N.*

window is clad with mirror instead of clear glass. This is an excellent example of the importance of placement of the mirror. Above eye level, it can be quite illusionary (see Figure 4.10).

The dining room of the Chateau de Rambouillet features the use of overmantel mirror and glass doors without muntins. Both elements amplify the spatial quality of the room (see Figure 4.11).

Figure 4.10 *Salon of the Bull's Eye, Palace of Versailles, France, late 17th century. © Photo R.M.N.*

Recent examples

The mirrored door with muntins is popular in hotel corridors, in combination with clear glass doors when symmetry is needed. In a similar vein, a couple in Washington, D.C., utilized a mirrored door with muntins next to a clear glass door, also with muntins. The glass door leads into a dining room and the mirrored door into the kitchen, which is

Figure 4.11 *The dining room in the Chateau de Rambouillet, France, 19th century. Courtesy of the French Government Tourist Office, New York.*

attractive but less decorative than the dining room. From the hallway, at first glance, both doors look like clear glass doors.

A Georgetown dressing/bathing room, designed in the 1980s, took motifs from the existing residence. The mirrored, paneled doors were copies of existing ones in the space. The remaining paneling was based on existing trim in the room. Additional storage was created above the tub in concealed doors, which were covered with wallpaper. The mirrors in the small room were less for vanity than to give a spatial expansion of the area, and to brighten it (see Figure 4.12).

There are many ways of achieving the look of muntins and mirror. The Appendix gives additional how-to information.

The clerestory window

We have seen that the panel above the door has a distinct history in design. In modern office buildings, mirror has, from time to time, been used above partitions to replicate clear glass windows—where the ceiling has been lowered for ducts, for instance. This is also effective in areas where people do not want to see themselves, but still wish a sense of space, such as in a home office or over a headboard.

Large Mirrored Surfaces

Mirrored walls or ceilings—or even, occasionally, mirrored floors—have the ability to transform the image of a space quickly. For these uses, the law of reflection is particularly important. Just what will be reflected in the mirror?

A cathedral for shoes

The I. Miller Shoe Salon in New York City, designed by Victor Lundy in 1962, is an excellent example of mirrored spatial enhancement of a commercial setting. The swooping ceiling, consisting of small strips of bent wood in a natural color, creates texture in the upper reaches of the space. (Reflections of ceilings with mirror can be a problem unless the ceilings have texture or similar embellishments.) Also, the space is dimly lighted which adds to its mysterious quality and reflections (see Figure 4.13).

Figure 4.12 *A Georgetown dressing/bathing room. Design: Pamela Heyne, 1986. Photo: William Mills.*

Figure 4.13 *I. Miller shoe salon, New York. Design: Victor Lundy, 1962. Photo: George Cserna.*

An entrance hall

Thomas Pheasant mirrored an entrance door for its spatial component, as well as its ability to bring light into the apartment from a distant window. He used strong contrasts of light and dark materials and strong forms to emphasize the sense of space in the mirrors. The bleached wood wall paneling and custom cabinets provide strong texture in the mirror (see Plate 28).

Another entrance hall

Mary Drysdale of Drysdale Design combined sheets of mirror with columns. It is often difficult to "stop" visually large expanses of mirror, but the columns are effective in this regard (see Figure 4.14).

Anatomy of a living room

A Georgetown living room, before being "remodeled" with mirrors by the author, was dark and narrow (see Figure 4.15).

The standard approach would have been to place a mirror over the mantel, and bookcases on either side of the fireplace. Here, however, it was decided to place mirrors on either side of the fireplace to emphasize the illusionary space in the mirrors. People who enter the space do not see their reflected image right away; thus, it makes the room seem all the larger. Additionally, if a mirror had been placed over the mantel, the reflection would not have been attractive: It would have been of the white drywall ceiling, and the radiator in the distance. So, mirrors were placed on either side of the fireplace rather than the more traditional flanking bookcases, standard for Georgetown.

The mirrors did reflect a few negative images. The mirror on the left-hand side reflected speakers; on the right-hand side, the mirrors reflected a distant computer, seen from around the corner in the mirrors (see Figures 4.16 and 4.17).

In both instances, simple screening devices were part of the equation. Plants, including a ficus tree, easily blocked the view of the speakers, and a table lamp blocked the view of the distant computer (see Plate 29).

Additionally, the ficus tree had a floor-mounted 50-watt spotlight to brighten the side next to the mirror, and to cast dramatic shadows on the ceiling which are duplicated in the mirrors. The reflection of plants and light give texture to the mirror and block the unattractive reflections.

Figure 4.14 Washington residence entrance hall.
Design: Drysdale Design. Photo: Mick Hales.

What about the joints? The largest possible size of mirror was determined by the size of the door entering the small Georgetown house. Hence, equal-sized panels were flanked by smaller panels. This emphasized the vertical dimension of the room.

Since clear mirror rather than ultra-clear mirror was selected, the existing peach-colored walls de-emphasized the naturally greenish color.

Figure 4.15 *Georgetown living room, initial condition. Photo: Pamela Heyne.*

Figure 4.16 Georgetown living room, in process. Note the reflection of the computer in the distance. This unattractive reflection was subsequently blocked with a table lamp (see Plate 29). Photo: Garrison Studio.

Figure 4.17 Law of reflection: The computer is visible in the mirror.

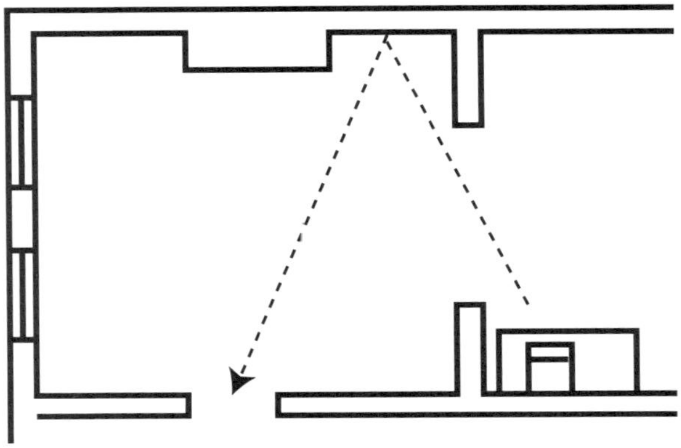

Other problem reflections

The Georgetown living room had some negative reflections that were mitigated by objects placed in front of the mirrors. However, sometimes the designer might be unpleasantly surprised by the reflections that appear from the outdoors. The hypothetical floor plan in Figure 4.18 is of a room that could be improved with mirrors. The owner wishes to maximize the reflection of trees in the mirrors. But where should the mirrors go?

The first reaction might be to place mirrors along the wall to the diagonal of the entrance. That placement, however, will result in an overwhelming reflection of what is just outside the window, a large brick wing jutting out from the building (see Figure 4.18a).

If mirrors are placed on the wall parallel to the line of travel, the maximum number of trees will be reflected in the mirror (see Figure 4.18b).

Small, unattractive reflections can be masked with lighting and plants, and even with furniture. However, it is best to have the overall reflection as beautiful as possible. If one has the option, duplicating trees is always preferable to duplicating unattractive, man-made objects.

A development project

Mirrors are used to enhance sales models in Oak Harbor and Grand Harbor, a high-end development, in Vero Beach, Florida. One of the bedrooms in the project has a wall-to-wall mirror installed over a built-in storage unit. The mirror reflects an arcaded porch and the view of water in the distance. The developers have doubled the view, and amplified space with simple means (see Figure 4.19).

Often, in development projects where large quantities of mirror are used, not enough attention is given to accessories adjacent to the mirrors. Accents, such as dramatic plants or boldly scaled patterns, can add impact. The Coventry Island dining room in Grand Harbor features large mirror squares, which reflect dramatic plants and the invitingly set table (see Figure 4.20).

Floating frames

Creating foreground interest on mirrors, such as hanging pictures, other mirrors—or even empty frames—is a way of heightening the sense of depth in the mirrors.

Figure 4.18 *Thorough planning of the mirror location will result in the most pleasing reflections.*

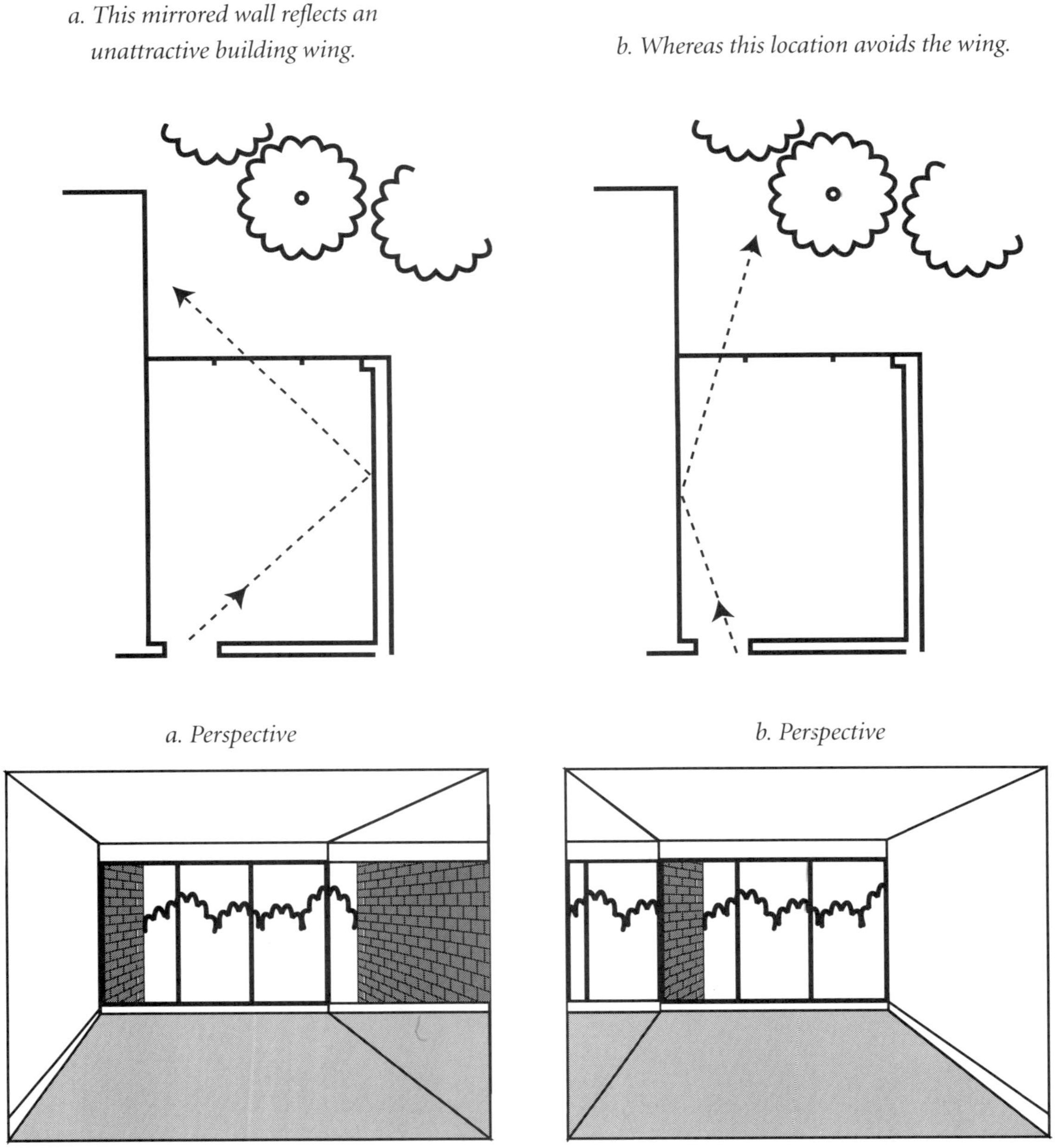

Thomas Pheasant has attached empty frames from Goldleaf Studios in Washington, D.C., atop a wall of mirror. The mirror was drilled prior to the installation of the frames. The frames, in turn, were painted black on the back, so as to not be visible. They give an intensity to the mirror, since the frames seem to be suspended in a mysterious fashion.

Figure 4.19 *Grand Harbor riverfront unit, Vero Beach, FL. Design: Betsy Godfrey. Photo: Doug Widell.*

Figure 4.20 *Coventry Island of Grand Harbor, Vero Beach, FL. Design: Betsy Godfrey. Photo: Doug Widell.*

Completing forms

A popular decorating solution to the narrow entrance hall is using a semicircular entrance table. Reflected in a mirror, of course, it looks like a full circle. This gives an illusionary boost to the often too-narrow space.

In an extremely narrow space in the Kips Bay Decorators' Showhouse in New York, Ron Bricke placed mirror adjacent to a semicircular window. The effect is a mirrored fooling of the eye, with the semicircular window becoming a full circular window. The dark woods also boost the illusion (see Plate 30).

Mirror can be particularly effective in showrooms and display areas where space is limited. In the Martin Albert showroom, Sam Botero placed a half-bed adjacent to a mirror. The swag above the bed and grouped pillows give the illusion of a full bed, without taking up the extra space in the showroom (see Figure 4.21).

Architect Charles Moore experimented with a semicircular domed ceiling, completed by mirror, at the Gund Investment Co. office in Princeton, New Jersey, in 1980. The mirror completed the form. A fascinating restaurant in Washington, D.C., is the City Café by David Schwarz. The architect scooped out a triangular well in the second floor. He then installed a mirror along one wall, turning the triangle into a square, all with the magic of mirrors (see Plate 31).

Mirror above eye level

Clyde's Restaurant in Washington, D.C., is a classic example of mirror as a means of enhancing space. Since the back, mirrored wall is angled away from the patrons, they do not see their own reflections when they first enter the space. When seated, people still do not see their reflections, since the backs of the booths were designed to be above head height. The mirrored panels are butted against the brick piers, giving a sense of depth. In addition, textures from brick walls, decorative lighting, plants, and skylight are reflected in the mirrors' depths (see Plate 32).

Mirrored ceilings

When mirroring the ceiling, it is important that the law of reflection be considered. A mirrored ceiling is most effective in simple spaces, such as entryways or dining rooms. Many years ago, the author saw in a design magazine a Manhattan dining room with a mirrored ceiling. The magazine has long been forgotten, but not the image of the mir-

Figure 4.21 *Martin Albert showroom. The mirror doubles the size of the bed. Design: Sam Botero Associates., Inc. Photo: Allec Hemer.*

rored ceiling, reflecting not only the glimmer of candles on the table, but also the view of the pinnacled city at night.

A word of caution: While a mirrored ceiling can be dramatic in a bathroom, the drama is lessened if it reflects a cluttered dressing table or the toilet and bidet. In other spaces, beware of what is on tabletops or what is on the walls. Even a series of small pictures on the wall can look busy if reflected in the ceiling.

The mirrored floor

In 1957, as part of the exhibit in Berlin entitled "America Builds," architect Peter Blake installed face-to-face mirrors as a means of showing the verticality of the U.S. skyscraper. He had a mockup of a segment of a curtain-wall building installed, then rimmed the top with a four-foot-wide strip of mirror, and placed a similar strip on the floor. People looked into the floor mirrors as if they were peering over an abyss. According to Blake, "They were getting woozy." A row of plants at the edge of the floor mirrors prevented the people from walking on the mirror.

The author once had a small dining room with one dramatic wall covering. Simple mirrored tiles at the intersection of wall and floor reflected the wall accent and gave the small space the element of surprise it needed. The space had minimal traffic, so a barrier was not necessary.

More Subtle Spatial Effects

Tinted mirrors

Tinted mirrors are created by silvering glass that has already been given some color. The most common colors are gray, bronze, green, blue, gold, peach, and pink. Black mirror is also available. A dimly lighted, crowded restaurant benefits from this subtle spatial material. A number of the examples in this book have walls of tinted mirror with clear glass mirror suspended in front of them. This can be quite illusionary, since one's reflection is less visible in the dark mirror. It has a feeling of dusk; the clear glass is a surprise over it.

Tinted mirrors make more of a statement than clear mirrors and must be carefully considered. Many designers use them as extensions of a given room's decor.

Gray mirrors, for instance, might form one wall of a gray hallway. Black-and-white prints could be mounted on top of the mirror. Some designers like gray mirror in conjunction with built-in cabinets. Houston designer Jan Kieta feels that gray mirror looks "more sophisticated" than plain mirror in custom cabinetry. Houston glass distributor Matt Forrest likes using gray mirror under white kitchen cabinets.

Bronze mirror is a particular favorite of Washington designer Veda Tiefel. She has placed bronze mirror in panels with custom gold trim, often with an accent of Venetian mirror on top of that. She favors deep hued walls and curtains, such as khaki, in combination with the bronze mirrors.

Gold mirror in large panels is popular in restaurants. It conveys a warm ambiance. A popular pizza chain uses gold mirror on most wall surfaces. It continues the tone of the warm colors throughout the restaurant—the rust-colored marble floor, natural wood surfaces, and pink neon accents in the bar area. The mirrors are flattering; perhaps patrons who feel they look healthy will feel better about eating a larger portion of pizza.

Pink and peach mirrors are also flattering. They have a long history of use in powder rooms and dressing rooms. These mirrors were often used as accents in Art Deco dressing tables and ladies' rooms.

Blue mirror is popular in Florida. It has obvious implications of water and a sense of coolness. Robert Dean used blue mirror as an accent in a soffit in a prototype Florida kitchen. An old coffee shop/restaurant in Washington, D.C., called "The Blue Mirror" had just that behind the counter. On a hot, steamy August day, the air conditioning in that restaurant, and the intense image of that mirror, provided instant physical and psychic relief.

Green mirror is not flattering to the human face, but can have applications in display or as part of a greenhouse wall, or used in conjunction with travertine marble or under cabinets.

Beveling

Beveling can convey a faceted, sparkling quality to mirror, and can help break up a large surface of mirror. The Mayflower Hotel in Washington has floor-to-ceiling panels of mirror, approximately 6 feet wide by 14 feet high. Rather than giving the effect of a single sheet of mirror, however, the facets pick up light and make the mirrors look more decorative.

Vertical mirror strips are a masking device that is particularly effective in small-scale locations. For instance, it might be desirable to give a sense of space without conveying exact reflections.

The author was asked to consult on mirror applications for the model homes in a low-cost townhome development in Washington. A particularly long, narrow entrance hall benefited from one-foot-wide strips of beveled mirror installed on one wall. It made the three-foot-wide hall seem wider. It also broke up the reflections of a powder room door.

Mirrors and lattice

Latticework has long been a popular device for gardens, garden rooms, and breakfast rooms. Outside, the lattice can provide a framework for a mirror, emphasizing space. The gazebo by Washington landscape architects Lawson/Carter conveys an illusionary view of green grass, looking as if the lawn continues rather than being simply a mirror blocking air conditioning equipment (see Figure 4.22).

Mirror with lattice can be quite illusionary. It can make an interior seem like a garden, and convey subtle reflections. Its placement is not as important as with clear mirror. When mirror is combined with lattice, the reflections of the viewer are minimized, since the lattice obscures the human form. Yet, the impression of space remains. The most common approach is to place crisscrossed lattice on top of sheets of mirror. The lattice must, of course, be attached to pieces of wood at the top and bottom of the mirror. Usually the lattice is painted white or a light color. Cutouts, such as oval or circular shapes, are common. Also, creating a diagonal effect with smaller strips of lattice leads the eye into an illusionary space. Both sides of the lattice must be painted, in this case, in order not to cast unfinished reflections in the mirrors. Since the lattice is on top of the mirror, reflections of the lattice are duplicated.

A different approach is found in the cocktail lounge at the Kennedy Center in Washington, D.C. Small pieces of mirror are inserted into rectilinear mahogany lattice. The lattice is not on top of the mirror; hence, it does not cast its own reflection in the mirror. These mirrors create a subtle spatial expansion and reflect elegant banquettes and regularly placed, silk-shaded lamps set at the edges of the banquettes.

Interestingly, when people are asked if they like the mirrors in the cocktail lounge, which has 20-foot-high walls covered in lattice and mirror, the response invariably is, "What mirrors?"

Figure 4.22 *Georgetown garden shows the use of lattice with mirror. Design: Lawson/Carter. Photo: Leslie Cashen.*

5

Dynamic Effects

"*The position* of looking glasses, with respect to the light and cheerfulness of rooms, was not well understood in England during the last century, although on the continent the effect of large mirrors had long been studied in certain places. Great advantage was in some cases taken by placing them obliquely, and in others by placing them opposite: Thus, new scenes and unexpected effects were often introduced."—Humphrey Repton, 1816 (Heyne, p. 11)

Humphrey Repton, the great 18th- and 19th-century British landscape architect, said that he discovered the effect of the oblique mirror by accident. He thought a builder had constructed a conservatory perpendicular to the main house, rather than parallel. Upon closer inspection, he realized that "a large looking glass, intended for the salon (which was not quite finished to receive it) had been accidentally placed in the green-house, at an angle of forty-five degrees, showing the conservatory in this manner. And I have since made occasional use of mirrors so placed to introduce views of scenery which could not otherwise be visible from a particular point of view." (Heyne, p. 13) Repton, who discovered the more sophisticated optical qualities of the mirror by accident, began using the mirror dynamically. For Repton, it became a tool to shift views at will.

With subtle combinations of mirrors or shifts in the mirrors' plane we can do far more than "make rooms seem bigger." In this section, we will see a variety of ways of using the mirror, ranging from the decorative to the pragmatic. The topics discussed will be:

- Multiple reflections, including infinity chambers
- Kaleidoscopes
- View shifting
- Periscopes
- The sun and the mirror

The examples are in different scales and have differing functions, yet have the same physical law underlying their use: the law of reflection.

Figure 5.1 *A magic trick, "The Living Half of a Woman": Mirrors at a 45-degree angle gave the illusion of transparency. From Hopkins,* Magic, *1901. Courtesy of the Library of Congress, Rare Book Division.*

A child will use the law of reflection intuitively. If a child in a sunny backyard is given a little pocket mirror, the child will instantly use it to obtain new views of flowers or shift sunbeams to dark corners.

Like the child, sometimes we are more concerned with the view in the mirror, and sometimes with the light itself that bounces off the mirror's surface. Bring a second or third mirror into the equation, and the views or light can be multiplied, shifted, and focused in a variety of ways. Parallel mirrors can be the basis of *glaces à repetition,* as used in French ballrooms. With transparent mirror and clear mirror, they can become an infinity chamber. Parallel mirrors placed at a 45-degree angle with respect to a window can suddenly become a periscope, conveying a beautiful exterior view to a dark basement.

The mirror at a 45-degree angle is important in cameras, in telescopes, for magic acts, in department store cooking demonstrations, and for designers as a means of conveying views not seen otherwise.

New Raisons d'Etre for the Mirror

It is estimated that the earth's total population will double within a generation, and will tend to cluster in urban regions, rather than being spread evenly over the globe. The result has been and will continue to be greater densities. Whereas our grandparents might have lived in a farmhouse with views of trees and grass from all the windows, our parents might have lived in a suburb with the views of neighbors' homes from most of the windows. We might now live in townhouses or apartments, with views from only one or two sides of the structure. Underground structures for shopping, academic facilities, sports facilities, museums, and offices are increasingly being used in regions where land is expensive, difficult to acquire, or simply unavailable.

Mirrors have an important function in making these environments more humane. Particularly in underground spaces, mirrors have many functions. They can make spaces brighter, dematerialize mass, convey views from around corners, shift views below grade via periscopes, or help to convey sunlight below grade. The heliostat, a tracking mirror, can provide intense sunlight throughout the day in underground areas.

The same heliostat, if mounted in an array, can produce incredibly high temperatures. However, heliostats and other forms of solar collectors are not in intensive use at this time. Electricity derived from solar collectors is approximately three times as expensive as that from fossil fuels. Additionally, governmental incentives to encourage solar collectors and other forms of renewable energy such as wind and thermal power have increasingly been eliminated. Nonetheless, we have seen as a society that economic and political forces can shift suddenly, giving new importance to renewable energy sources. Also, it seems obvious that, at some point, we will simply run out of fossil fuels. Therefore, it seems worthwhile to have a general understanding of alternatives. In recent years designers have devised numerous ingenious solutions for intensifying or focusing sunlight, or simply for saving energy.

Tremendous energy can be saved by using the power of reflection. A mirror adjacent to a bathroom or kitchen light will double the light emitted. Light shelves—horizontal panels placed near the upper reaches of windows—can increase daylight to a space, particularly if reflective materials such as mirror are placed on the top of those shelves. Mirror lining skylight wells can result in greater light output, necessitating a smaller opening. This has been the basis of the SunPipe™ skylight, which uses a highly reflective interior: a 13-inch-diameter pipe that produces the equivalent of 15 100-watt bulbs, eliminating the need for electric lights during the day.

Multiple Reflections

The designer who places two mirrors face to face, then hangs a chandelier between the two mirrors, knows, intuitively, that the light from the chandelier will bounce onto the mirrors, and continue to bounce from mirror to mirror. This bouncing of light produces the effect of infinity.

Since the end of the 17th century, when mirrors improved in quality, designers have placed mirrors face to face or in arcs, or rimmed spaces with them to create varied effects. We have seen the darkly sumptuous Hotel Beauharnais bathroom, and modern bathing areas rimmed with clear or tinted mirror. The exuberantly rococo Amalienburg Pavilion derived a portion of its festive atmosphere from the reflection of windows in the mirrors, and the reflection of candles (see Figure 1.21). In the book, *The Decoration of Houses*, Edith Wharton wrote of multiple reflections: "The old French decorators relied upon the reflection of mirrors for producing an effect of distance in the treatment of gala rooms. Above the mantel, there was always a mirror with another of the same shape and size directly opposite; and the glittering perspective thus produced gave to the scene an air of fantastic unreality." (Wharton, Codman, p. 141).

The infinity chamber

The infinity chamber also has an air of "fantastic unreality," because we see small pinpoint lights cascading into infinity; yet, unlike the gala room, we do not see our own reflection. This is because we are standing on the outside looking in. We are looking through a transparent mirror to a grid of small decorative lights mounted on clear mirror. The transparent mirror and decorative mirror may be six inches apart. The light bounces from mirror to mirror, creating a dazzling effect. These have been popular decorative cubes or displays for hotels and restaurants.

In the late 1970s, Paul Rudolph experimented with infinity chambers, incorporating them into bookcases (see Figure 5.2) and even creating large, wall-size panels. Rudolph used lights in rectilinear patterns. One can imagine a basement dining room with a festive and infinite sense of space, created by an array of infinity chambers.

Figure 5.2 *Infinity chamber. Design: Paul Rudolph, 1978. Photo: Robert Perron.*

Light sculptures

Another form of multiple reflections are the light sculptures created by artist Rockne Krebs. The approach here is not to create a sense of infinite space, but to bounce laser beams from mirror to mirror. Krebs has executed these laser pieces on interiors and in exterior spaces, some as vast as the Mall in Washington, D.C. The effect is a complex series of crisscrossing streams of light. On the exterior pieces, the mirrors are installed in buildings and in distant trees. The angles are carefully calculated by the artist (see Figure 5.3).

Figure 5.3 *Laser light sculpture, Philip M. Stern House, Washington, DC. Design and photo: Rockne Krebs.*

Amusing displays

Multiple reflections can result in whimsical displays. The Museum of Science and Technology in Chicago features a section on human perception. The entrance to that exhibit is a corridor, lined with distorted mirrors on both sides.

At the turn of the century, when entire walls of mirror were unusual, funhouses might install such walls at 60-degree angles. A group of several people would enter the three-sided room and, by moving their arms, become a raging crowd (see Figure 5.4).

Figure 5.4 *Multiple reflections amused crowds in turn-of-the-century fairs and amusement parks. From Hopkins,* Magic, *1901. Courtesy of the Library of Congress, Rare Book Division.*

Kaleidoscope

Mirrors placed at 60-degree angles were the basis of an amusing funhouse display that delighted visitors at the turn of the century. They are also the basis of many kaleidoscopes that delight and fascinate today. While the kaleidoscope has generally been thought of as a portable element, it also has potential as an architectural feature.

The kaleidoscope creates a series of geometric patterns because of the reflection in an array of mirrors of shifting pieces of colored glass, stones, feathers, or colored liquids at the remote end of the scope. The kaleidoscope was invented by a Scottish inventor, Sir David Brewster (1781-1868).

A child prodigy, Brewster entered the University of Edinburgh when he was 12 years old. Although he was interested in mathematics, his family had hoped he would become a preacher. However, it was not his calling:

> *He was licensed, but the first day he mounted the pulpit was the last—for he had then, if he has not still, a nervous something about him that made him swither when he heard his own voice and saw a congregation eyeing him; so he sticked his discourse and vowed never to try that job again. It was a pity for the Kirk, but it was a good day for science....for if the doctor had gotten a manse, he might most likely have taken to his toddy like other folk.* (James Hogg, as quoted by Baker, p. 10)

Brewster had a stellar career as scientist, writer, inventor, philosopher, and editor of the Edinburgh Encyclopedia. He received numerous awards, and was knighted by King William IV. Yet, his most well-known accomplishment was a device that appealed to scientists and common people alike. In 1816, he invented the kaleidoscope, to great popular acclaim. Two years later, in *Blackwood's Magazine,* Dr. Roget said,

> *In the memory of man, no invention, and no work, whether addressed to the imagination or to the understanding, ever produced such an effect. A universal mania for the instrument seized all classes, from the lowest to the highest, from the most ignorant to the most learned, and every person not only felt, but expressed the feeling, that a new pleasure had been added to their existence.* (Baker, p. 14)

Although the kaleidoscope soon became an international success, Brewster received little financial remuneration for the invention.

The typical kaleidoscope array consists of three angled mirrors or two angled mirrors and a third side painted black. The end of the scopes, or object ends, have various colored objects—they can be rotating colored glass wheels, blown feathers, crystals, colored liquids in suspension, or views of the outside world. As the images at the ends of the scope change, the patterns created by the mirrors change (see Figure 5.5).

The three-mirror scopes produce the effect of a continuous tapestry of images. The two-mirror scopes produce a central image, the shape varying depending on the angle of the mirrors (see Figure 5.6).

Figure 5.5 *Diagram of kaleidoscopes by Shel Haber. From* Kaleidoscope Renaissance *by Cozy Baker. Reprinted by permission.*

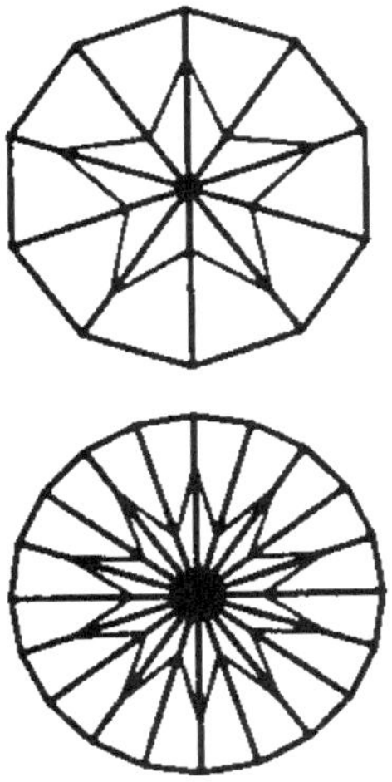

Figure 5.6 *Examples of symmetry created with two mirrors. From* Kaleidoscope Renaissance *by Cozy Baker. Reprinted by permission.*

Mirror Arrangements

Angle	*Symmetry*	*Image*
60 degrees	6-fold symmetry	3-point star
45 degrees	8-fold symmetry	4-point star
36 degrees	10-fold symmetry	5-point star
30 degrees	12-fold symmetry	6-point star
22.5 degrees	16-fold symmetry	8-point star
20 degrees	18-fold symmetry	9-point star
18 degrees	20-fold symmetry	10-point star
15 degrees	24-fold symmetry	12-point star

Source: Kaleidoscope Renaissance by Cozy Baker. Reprinted by permission.

Variations are considerable. Four-mirror systems produce square or rectilinear patterns, often with a striped effect. Cylindrical tubes will produce a spiraling effect, and tapered tubes will produce a spherical, three-dimensional effect when viewed from the larger end. Additionally, polyangular arrangements allow the two-mirror effects to be varied by allowing the viewer to change the angles of the mirrors. Some have also experimented with two or more mirrored systems in a given "scope" with separate eyepieces. (Baker, p. 38)

Bruce Haney, an Omaha, Nebraska, investment counselor with a great interest in kaleidoscopes, decided to create an architecturally scaled kaleidoscope, combining the kaleidoscope with a skylight. Under a standard domed skylight, he created a three-sided well with four-foot-long tapered mirrors, mounted to industrial boards. Just under the skylight itself he placed a light bulb, for nighttime use. Next, he placed two stained glass rotating wheels (rotating in opposite directions for maximum variation in reflections) to give the kaleidoscope its color and pattern. In essence, he created a large 60-degree kaleidoscope. Rather than straight sides, however, it has canted sides, which produce the circular pattern in his kaleidoscope.

How do you change the light bulb? Simple: You go on to the roof and remove the domed skylight. However, according to Haney, long-life bulbs make this factor less bothersome.

Haney calls it the "through the roof" kaleidoscope because, he says jokingly, that was his wife's reaction when he mentioned his idea to her (see Plate 33).

One could imagine this as being particularly delightful over a bed, where one could look at the ever-changing patterns with ease. In this case, it was placed over the dining room table. How, then, is it possible to see the patterns without craning your neck during dinner? Simple: a small custom-made mirrored pyramid sits in the center of the dining room table and conveys faceted views of the kaleidoscope to the diners (see Figure 5.7).

The rotating stained glass wheels were made by Ward Robinson, a local kaleidoscope maker. The lower stained glass wheel was made in a cone shape to hide the upper supports of the mirrors. However, this is not what results in the glorious circular patterns; that is a result of the tapered mirrors.

Figure 5.7 *Table-top kaleidoscope viewer. Design and photo: Bruce Haney.*

Therapeutic value of kaleidoscopes

Gazing at the kaleidoscope has been shown to have a therapeutic value to people in stressful situations. The shifting colors and constantly changing beautiful abstract patterns help people focus on the images in the kaleidoscope rather than on their personal problems.

In particular, the circular images give a sense of a mandala, the circular form found in ancient creation myths symbolizing unity and wholeness in life. In an Indian creation myth, the god Brahma stands in the center of an enormous thousand-pointed lotus and looks in four directions. In another myth, Buddha steps onto an enormous lotus at the moment of birth and looks in all directions.

The kaleidoscope's mandala is constantly changing. Out of one mandala, a new mandala emerges.

It is perfection created from disparate and chaotic elements. The materials in themselves have no pattern, yet, when viewed in the eyepiece, the reflection of the mirrors creates a symbol of perfection. Psychotherapist Jeannie Robertson (quoted in Baker, p.47) uses the kaleidoscope as a symbol of affirmation:

Life unfolds from the center
New beginnings emerge from the breakup of past forms
All things turn and spin and change
Endlessly rearranging themselves
The world is truly a kaleidoscope

Kaleidoscopes have always been a source of delight. The Brewster Society, an international society of kaleidoscope enthusiasts and inventors, was founded by Potomac, Maryland, resident Cozy Baker, who has more than 1,000 kaleidoscopes in her home. Mrs. Baker has appeared on television as an inspiration to many. After the death of her son, she began looking at kaleidoscopes as a way of giving herself solace. Eventually this form of therapy became a fascinating vocation. She wrote the first book on kaleidoscopes, has founded a network of those with like interests, and organized one of the first exhibits of kaleidoscopes.

View Shifting

The "shifty-eyed" person is synonymous with one who is tricky or deceptive. The mirror that shifts views can either be a tool or an architectural device to bring unexpected views to an environment.

The mirror as a tool

The mirror that shifts views, such as the car's side view mirror, can literally be a lifesaver. In World War I, the trench mirror was an important device that enabled soldiers crouching in a trench to see opponents across the field. It was a small metal mirror, approximately 1½ inches by 1½ inches, with a metal loop on the end so that the mirror could be hooked onto the end of a bayonet and shift the view to the eyes of the soldier. This is also the basis for cameras and telescopes that use the mirror at a 45-degree angle to shift views to various eyepieces, and is the basis for mirrors placed above chefs in department-store cooking demonstrations.

The wall-mounted convex mirror, placed at the entrance of parking garages and in driveways, helps motorists tell if other cars are nearby. We have seen that dome or convex mirrors help day care centers keep track of some of the children under the care of the center. They are also important to ward off accidents in industrial settings where people are moving quickly in corridors. In sales areas, they help prevent crime.

Even the most decorative of convex girandole mirrors fascinated observers in 18th- and 19th-century drawing rooms because of the miniaturized views available.

Today it is possible to purchase a mirrored device invented by Benjamin Franklin called the "Philadelphia Busybody." An unobtrusive device of angled mirrors and copper backing designed to sit just outside a window, it lets the occupants of an upper floor in a house know the identity of a person knocking at the door.

While we do not often associate churches with mirrors, mirrors are often used in these settings to assist the organist, who might double as choirmaster. Organist Michael Lindstrom reminisced about an early church experience. He and the choir were both on a second-floor balcony. He was seated at the organ with his back to the altar. Although the organ was elegantly and richly carved, as he put it, an old "truck mirror" was planted on the side so that he could witness what was happening at the altar. In another church setting, Christ Church in Georgetown, Mr. Lindstrom's post flanked the altar. He noted that large mirrors were placed under a Gothic arch near the altar so that some of the choir, whose back was to him, could see his directions. The mirrors helped the organist, in one instance, see what was happening during the service; in another instance, it helped part of the choir to see him.

We have seen how in the philosophy of feng shui, view shifting is very important. Not only are mirrors used to redirect forces, but they are also valuable as a device to see if an intruder is lurking. Mirrors are often placed in bedrooms to enable those in bed to see if someone is at the entrance of the room. If the occupant cannot see the door directly, the mirror can assist in this regard.

Decorative applications

We have seen subtle tilts of mirror throughout the book. Frankie Welch tilted a wall mirror in her dining room slightly sideways, imperceptibly, to improve the reflection. The Barista Brava Coffee Shop in Washington features mirrors tilted slightly forward. The mirrors, thus, do not emphasize the spatial illusions in the room, but become charming accents, reflecting the comings and goings in the busy little space, as well as the coffee makers and elegantly displayed foodstuffs. Although the designers could very well have inserted the mirror in the arches, they chose not to have the mirror disappear, but to make it a dominant feature in the space (see Plate 14).

Charles Gandy used an angled mirror to emphasize the views of some small-scale handcrafted pottery. Called "the Julia Child mirror," it was placed on struts above the brightly colored pottery, and tilted at an angle to permit the viewers to see the backs and tops of the items. His jocular title was based on the angled mirrors one often sees in cooking demonstrations (see Plate 34).

A particularly elegant mantelpiece was created by Richar Interiors. A mirror that can be tilted is an intriguing new take on the overmantel mirror (see Plate 35).

Recently, the mode of simply resting a tall mirror against the wall has become popular. For some designers, this is part of the "trashed palazzo" look, which implies that one comes from vast resources and ancient lineage, and can thus afford to be casual about one's inherited possessions.

The leaning mirror is popular with designers of more minimalist persuasion. Philippe Starck placed leaning mirrors in the bedrooms of the Delano Hotel in Miami. Their function is to convey the view of the room's occupant, as well as conveying unexpected images of the room. Also, the mirror is treated as a piece of sculpture.

Views of the Outdoors

DESKTOP VIEW SHIFTER

View shifting is a wonderful means to convey views of the exterior to a windowless wall. The author created a simple desktop view shifter to transport views from the outside into the room. Since the mirror is typically at a 45-degree angle, the person seated at the desk does not see his or her own reflection but, instead, the image of the outdoors (see Plate 2).

MIRRORED SHUTTERS

Other useful devices for view shifting are mirrored shutters, which can be particularly useful if a view directly outside the window is not wonderful, such as in an alley. Mirrored shutters will convey oblique views of the outdoors. In addition, they are often less expensive to construct than custom-made drapery would be, and at night, if closed, they can provide additional energy savings and a measure of security. The best way to apply mirror on shutters is to have a bi-fold arrangement, so that the mirror does not end up on the outside when the shutter is closed. At night, then, one would be looking not at a black window, but at a reflection of the brightly lit interior. It is important that the mirrors be installed vertically. In older houses, the carpenter might have to compensate for crooked window jambs.

WINDOW JAMBS

A similar approach would be to mirror the inside of deep-set window jambs or mullions. This has been a popular approach in rooftop dining rooms to dematerialize the vertical mullions.

Gunnar Birkerts used mirror on window jambs in the upper levels of a law library at the University of Michigan, a portion of which was underground. The jambs convey oblique views of the surrounding Gothic architecture, as well as sun and sky, to students working on lower-level balconies.

Door jambs

Antony Childs, a Washington designer, often mirrored the insides of large-scale door jambs, leading from one room to another. He noted that, in social situations, sometimes the views could be amusing.

Mirrors on adjacent walls

Mirrors can be installed outdoors, perpendicular to an existing window, to convey an oblique view. This is particularly effective in townhouse settings. This could be something as simple as inexpensive framed mirrors, randomly placed on a brick wall outside a window.

View shifter windows

Using the magician's 45-degree mirror, a custom bay window can mitigate the negative views of the typical suburban side yard. The author designed her first view shifter window for a photographer and his wife, Bill and Helen Mills. The window was cantilevered from the side of the house. Unlike a typical bay window, one of the angled walls was solid, designed to accept a mirror. The couple had to decide which view they would prefer seeing in the mirror: the verdant backyard facing north, or the view of the suburban street on the south. They chose the southern exposure, feeling that the additional sunlight would be a boon to the dark, central dining room. In the long run they have been pleased with that decision, for their two daughters enjoyed playing in the sunny window. The sunlight had been amplified by the mirrors (see Plates 36 and 37).

The angled window worked extremely well for another client, Diane Borngesser, who had a beautiful river view from the rear of her house, but an uninspiring view of her neighbors' gray siding next door. The angled bay window conveyed the view of water to the center of her home—in this case, the entrance hallway.

A more dramatic approach to the view shifter window would be to have the angled wall with mirror extend totally in front of the existing opening, which will totally block out the view next door. However, it results in a greater extension beyond the existing window, thereby probably necessitating foundations rather than a simple cantilever.

Skylights

Skylights are often rimmed with mirrors, which redirect views of sky and clouds to people below. Additionally, the mirrors substantially increase the amount of light conveyed by the skylights and make the shaft less oppressive.

Periscope

The periscope is another form of view shifting, yet it requires two mirrors to shift the views. The mirrors must be parallel and placed at a 45-degree angle to the view. As the distance is increased between the upper and lower mirrors, lenses will be required to expand the light. In most instances, the view is shifted from above ground to below ground. The periscope in submarines shifted views from above the ocean to the bottom of a narrow viewing tube. Periscopes can also shift views from below ground to above ground; this was the approach in Shakespearean England. Periscopes have been known since Shakespeare's time, with stage ghosts being created with angled mirror below stage, shooting an image of the actor above the stage through a trap door to another piece of angled clear glass.

An interior residential periscope

As is typical of millions of homes in the United States, Bill and Helen Mills (the clients with the first view shifter window, now relocated to a larger home and game for another experimental window) had a dark, uninteresting basement. The main window in the basement, facing north, was high with a view of the underside of shrubbery. The author suggested constructing a periscope window at the unattractive north window. Some initial preparation was necessary. The Millses removed the high shrubbery in order to obtain a more pleasing long view of their front yard. Although it was not mandatory, they installed a new fixed glass window, which emphasized the exterior view.

In order to make the window as illusionary as possible, the "mechanics" of the device were concealed. In other words, the angled upper mirror was concealed so that only the lower, illusionary mirror would be seen. The upper mirror, attached to ¾" plywood, was supported by a drywall arch and intermediate beam that spanned the arch. Rather than looking at the back of an angled mirror, the arch was "filled in" in the front with a plywood panel. Additionally, a fluorescent light was installed in that area, as well as a venetian blind. With any shifting device, it must be remembered that at night the view of the person working at the desk can just as easily be shifted upward.

The Millses' two children, teenagers by this time, loved the periscope window, and vied with each other as to who would get to do their homework sitting near it. The effect is slightly surrealistic, as one sees the "tunnel," the walls between the two mirrors.

It is important that both the upper and lower mirrors be accessible for cleaning. A built-in desk in front of them would have made this mundane task more difficult than the solution devised: a desk on casters, easily removed when necessary.

Figure 5.8 *The Millses' basement before work began. Photo: William Mills.*

The window is highly illusionary. Many, upon first seeing it, assume it is a real window, and that somehow "a hole had been knocked in the wall." This periscope is a cosmetic retrofit of an existing opening. To rebuild the opening and scoop out a subterranean courtyard in front of the window would have been much more expensive, and would have resulted in a subterranean view rather than the expansive view obtained of lawn and flowers and the houses across the street.

It is important that the mirrors be as parallel as possible. No sagging should exist in the plywood or in the mirrors; thus, adequate structural supports must exist in conjunction with the plywood. The upper mirror, besides having mechanical attachments, should have a mastic attachment as well. (See Figures 5.8 and 5.9 and Plate 38.)

Figure 5.9 *Periscope window in process. Photo: William Mills.*

An exterior residential periscope

The dark areaway is another problem area in modern basements, with the window to an areaway looking out onto a concrete or brick wall. An exterior periscope could easily mitigate the negatives of this situation. One angled mirror could be installed outside of the areaway, and the second one would be inside the areaway at the bottom. The mirrors would have to be waterproofed, possibly with a clear glass covering.

Other periscopes

In similar fashion, the Corning Museum of Glass in Corning, New York, designed by Gunnar Birkerts and completed in 1980, features a linear exterior periscope. The view is shifted from the lower angled mirror to the upper angled mirror, placed on the "eyebrow."

Figure 5.10 *Section view of the Corning Museum of Glass. Periscope shifts view to upper mirror. Design: Gunnar Birkerts, 1980.*

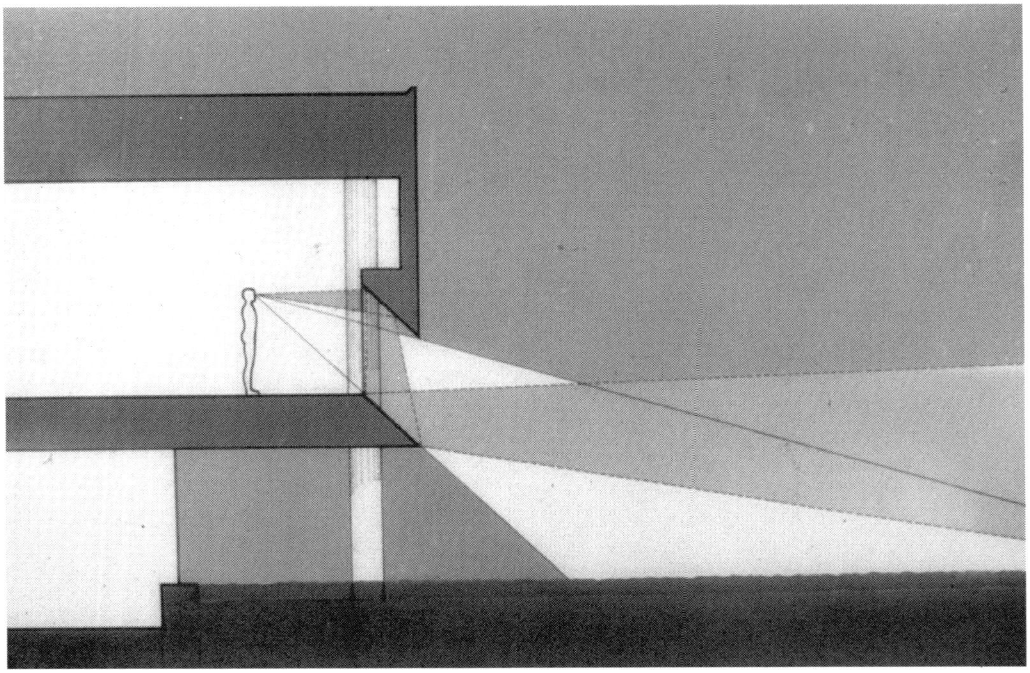

The glass is shielded from the direct rays of the sun, yet the mirror conveys views of the exterior to the patrons inside the museum. The view on the upper mirror is ambiguous and partly shielded by draperies in the museum (see Figure 5.10).

Another version of the linear periscope is in the Fort Snelling Visitor Center in Minneapolis, Minnesota, designed by BRW Architects and finished in 1983. Workers can receive a view of the exterior courtyard from two stories below grade. According to Stephen Osman, an executive in charge of the facility, there is no distortion with the periscope, but cleaning it is not an easy task; hence, the mirrors tend to get dirty. When asked if people were happy with the periscope windows, he replied that they were "as reasonably happy as people can be that don't have a *real* window. It's something, at least." (See Figure 5.11.)

Figure 5.11 *Fort Snelling Visitor's Center. Design: BRW Architects, 1983. From* Underground Space Design, *Carmody/Sterling.*

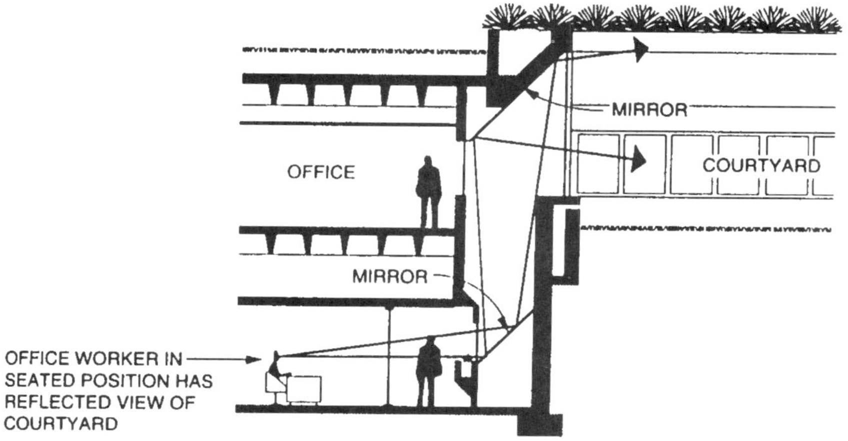

A larger and more complex version of the periscope is located at the Civil and Mineral Engineering Building at the University of Minnesota, also by BRW Architects, constructed in 1983. The periscope is located in a narrow shaft, and the light is intensified by a series of lenses interspersed throughout the shaft. The view is conveyed 100 feet below grade to an office area. The shaft for the periscope was adjacent to another shaft for a heliostat, conveying sunlight to the same location.

John Carmody worked in the space for 12 years as associate director of the Underground Space Center, which was located there. He wrote of the periscope, "Here the designers chose to maximize the depth or three-dimensional aspect of the image but at the expense of only seeing it from one position. Thus it lacks the feeling of a window that is seen from different places in a room and is used more like a periscope on a submarine. People must go to the viewing position to receive information about the exterior." (Carmody, p. 251) Carmody, now on the architecture faculty at the University of Minnesota, said that the periscope was less significant to the workers in the underground offices than the sunlight, which was intense throughout the day. When asked if he had found working underground depressing, he said it was not, partly because of the open, airy design and contact with sunlight, and partly because of abundant activity in the offices. He mentioned that people working in department stores experience minimal depression since the environment is typically lively and stimulating (see Figure 5.12).

The periscope window is still an experimental form. In the case of the Mills window, the desk was adjacent to the mirrors and wonderful intimate views of flowers and distant lawns were possible. In the case of the Fort Snelling periscope and the periscope at the University of Minnesota, viewers were more remote from the outdoors, and from the mirrors.

The Sun and the Mirror

Sunlight is free, plentiful energy, but it is diffuse. Mirrors can focus sunlight to intensify its energy at a given point or along a line (see Figure 5.13).

Early humans used the burning mirror to create fire. Concave obsidian could create fires; concave metal mirrors could as well. As glass technology improved, glass lenses also were used to create fires. These hand-held devices obviously had great importance to the survival of our earliest ancestors.

Figure 5.12 *Periscope and heliostat in the Civil and Mineral Engineering Building, University of Minnesota. Design: BRW Architects, 1983. Heliostat design: Shimizu Corp. From* Underground Space Design, *Carmody/Sterling.*

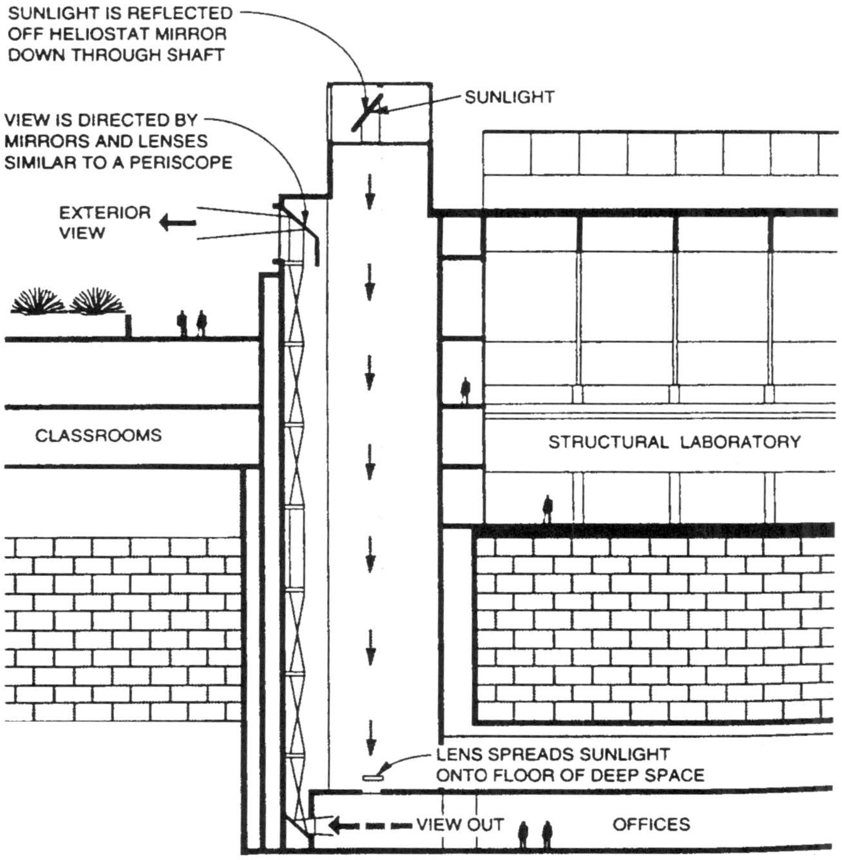

Archimedes was reported to have used mirrors to redirect sunlight and create a conflagration in Roman vessels during the siege of Syracuse by Marcellus. Numerous experiments with this over the years have shown that Archimedes may well have been successful.

Over the years, a variety of solar devices, such as solar cookers and solar engines, as well as means of producing steam, electricity, and high temperatures have proven useful.

Figure 5.13 *Dello Specchio da Fuoco, from Fine, Opere di Orontio Fineo del Delfinato, 1587. Courtesy of the Library of Congress, Rare Book Division.*

Dello Specchio da Fuoco. 13

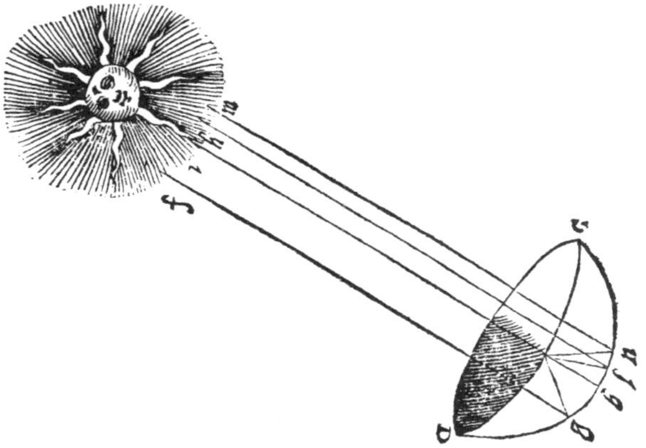

Vantaggio III.

Di più ſi raccoglie ancora, che lo Specchio di queſta tal forma, cioè cauato ſecondo il taglio Parabola del Cono diritto, & dirittangolo, è del più intenſo, & più preſto accendimento, che qual ſi voglia altro Specchio propoſto. Imperoche non ſi truoua niuno altro Specchio, eccetto che il ſopraſcritto parabolico: che dalla total ſuperficie di quello i raggi del Sole ſi ritorchino in vn ſol punto comune. Et ſe alcun'altro Specchio ſi poteſſe ritrouar tale, egli principalmente ſarebbe l'hemisferico concauo: Ma in lui ſi trouano tanti punti di ripiegamenti, quanti ſono i riuolgimenti in cerchio de' raggi cadenti: come ſi conoſce facilmente per Vitellione, & altri Auttori, che ſcriuono di Perſpettiua. Solo adunque lo Specchio fabricato ſecondo il taglio Parabola del Cono diritto, & dirittangolo, ha vn punto; nel quale comunemente ripercuoteno i cadenti raggi del Sole: Et conciosiacoſa che la virtù vnita ſia più gagliarda della ſeparata, auuiene, che per lo comune concorſo de' ripiegati raggi di quello s'accenda più toſto, & con maggior gagliardezza in eſſo Specchio parabolico ſopra dimoſtrato, che per qual ſi voglia altro Specchio propoſto.

Solar mirrors

Solar mirrors take a variety of forms, ranging from simple to sophisticated.

Simple reflective flaps operated by a winch can heat water tanks (see Figure 5.14). A reflective canted wall on a solar greenhouse can also heat a container of water. Heliostats in American desert areas focus sunlight toward power towers to create steam, which can, in turn, generate electricity. At the solar furnace at Odeillo in the French Alps, heliostats focus solar energy toward a power tower and can create temperatures of over 2000 degrees Fahrenheit. These high temperatures are used to fuse metals without contamination.

Figure 5.14 *Vacation house in Carlyle, Illinois, has reflective flaps that open to intensify heat into solar collectors. Design: Michael Jantzen, 1978. Courtesy of* Today's Architectural Mirror.

Maximizing light

Mirrors can intensify ordinary electric light when used in conjunction with fixtures, and can also amplify sunlight. Indeed, Iranian cut mirrorwork was designed to amplify light in glittering fashion in shrines and palaces.

A simple example might be called "chasing sunbeams." The author noticed a beam of sunlight in a stairwell at home. A portable framed mirror was quickly installed at that spot. Then, another mirror was placed where that beam landed, and a third mirror placed at the bottom of the stair. With the simple act of installing three strategically placed mirrors, the hallway soon became flooded with a golden afternoon light. Obviously, these mirrors were not "tracking" the sun. Since they were small, the effect was short-lived. Yet, it demonstrated the power and potential beauty of reflected light.

Figure 5.15 *Residential kitchen, before installation of 13-inch SunPipe™. Courtesy of SunBox® Co.*

The light pipe

The light pipe is a means of redirecting light in confined spaces. This type of skylight does not permit views of clouds and blue sky, but it has numerous advantages nonetheless. An example is the SunPipe™, which reflects daylight down a tube that is 13 inches in diameter, with a maximum practical length of 20 feet (see Figures 5.15 and 5.16). Beyond this length, a 21-inch-diameter SunPipe is recommended (see Figures 5.17 and 5.18). The advantages of this design are speed and ease of installation, maximization of light, and minimizing excess heat gain or loss. The light is spread out at the base of the tube with a translucent ceiling lens.

Figure 5.16 *Kitchen after installation of 13-inch SunPipe™. Courtesy of SunBox® Co.*

Figure 5.17 *Office environment, before installation of 21-inch SunPipe™. Courtesy of SunBox® Co.*

Figure 5.18 *Office after installation of 21-inch SunPipe™. Courtesy of SunBox® Co.*

Sun scoops and light shelves

At the Famolare Shoe Company, the architects Banwell, White and Arnold placed mirrors outside a clerestory window. The mirrors were adjusted twice a year to conform to the angles of the sun (see Figure 5.19). The mirrors created "splashes of light" on the wall of the atrium. The average person entering the space had no idea that the sunlight was amplified by mirrors.

Figure 5.19 *Mirrors on the roof reflect light into a clerestory window. Design: Banwell, White and Arnold.*

New developments in light reflection include stationary Fresnel lenses placed outside clerestories, redirecting light to other reflective materials, including mirrors placed at a 45-degree angle.

Light shelves have also become a significant means of redirecting natural light (see Figure 5.20).

Figure 5.20 *Illustration of light shelf and skylights combined to maximize daylight. From* Underground Space Design, *Carmody/Sterling.*

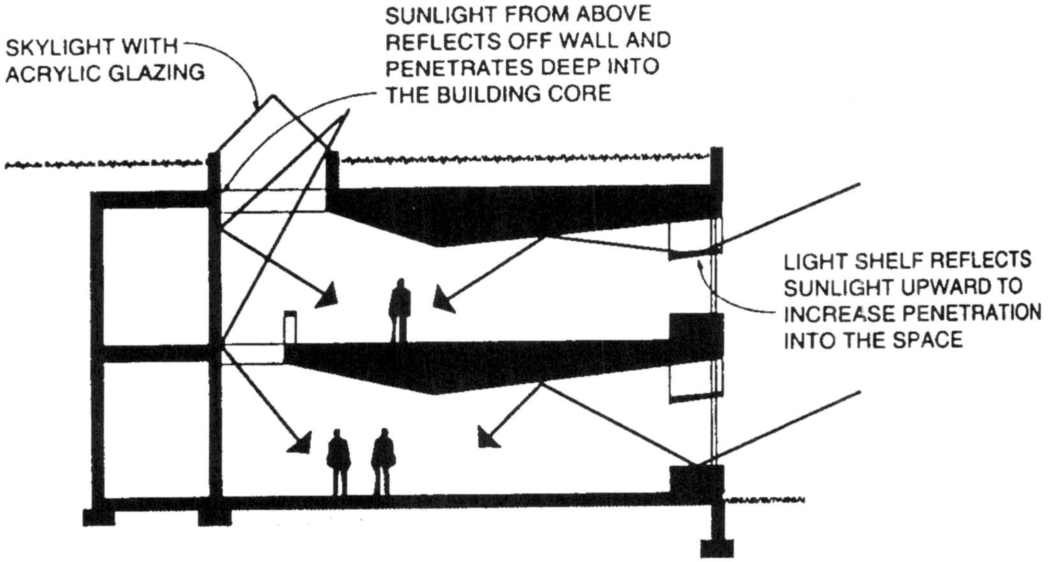

Heliostats

We have seen the importance of the heliostat in conveying sunlight to the subterranean offices at the University of Minnesota. The heliostat gave workers a link to the outdoors, resulting in a more cheerful atmosphere. Heliostats have also been used in large offices with central atriums. "In the Hong Kong Bank building, natural light is provided to a 10-story atrium by a system of reflecting mirrors. Overhead skylights are not possible since the atrium only occupies the lower floors of the tall building. A large movable reflector panel on the side of the building directs sunlight to an array of mirrors on the atrium ceiling that reflect the light downward." (Carmody, p. 273) Heliostats have also been used in conjunction with light pipes (see Figure 5.21).

Future Reflections

The mirror is hypothesized by some as a means of helping to solve future energy needs in ever more dramatic ways. Orbiting mirrors redirecting solar energy to terrestrial conversion sites could "augment and possibly even replace the present electrical generating capacity of the world." (Goldberg, p. 234) While it sounds farfetched, the Russians have recently redirected solar energy to northern regions of the globe from a Mir spacecraft.

The Hubble telescope, a glass instrument, was recently installed in space to see farther than previously possible, without the interference of the earth's atmosphere. It is truly amazing that the small device that helped our ancestors create fires and see images of themselves today helps us improve our environments in ever more imaginative ways, and gives us increasingly new insights, about ourselves and about our very universe.

Figure 5.21 Sunlight from a rooftop heliostat mounted 110 feet above. Civil and Mineral Engineering Building, University of Minnesota. Design: BRW Architects. Photo: John Carmody. From Underground Space Design.

Appendix: Mirror Installation and Cleaning

Installation of Framed Mirrors

Framed mirrors, unless they are quite small, should not be installed with a wire and a single nail or hook. The recommended approach is to have two steel strap hangers mounted on either side of the frame. The strap hangers can then be attached to the wall with two horizontal screws, molly bolts or double brad hangers. Often, a loop of wire is attached to the steel strap (see Figure A.1).

Installation of Wall Mirrors

After careful measuring and cutting of the mirrors in the shop, small clips should be installed at the bottom of the wall to support the mirrors. The upper portion of the mirrors can be attached with various trims, or mastic, appropriate to the backing and wall. (It is best if the worker use a dropcloth when applying mastic.) Finally, the mirrors can be installed and carefully adjusted to make sure reflections are vertical (see Figures A.2, A.3, and A.4).

Figure A.1 *Means of attaching framed mirror. Courtesy of the North American Association of Mirror Manufacturers.*

Figure A.2 J-clips attached to the wall to support the bottom of the mirrors. Courtesy of Columbia Glass and Mirror.

Figure A.3 Application of mastic on the rear of the mirror.

Figure A.4 Final alignment of mirrors.

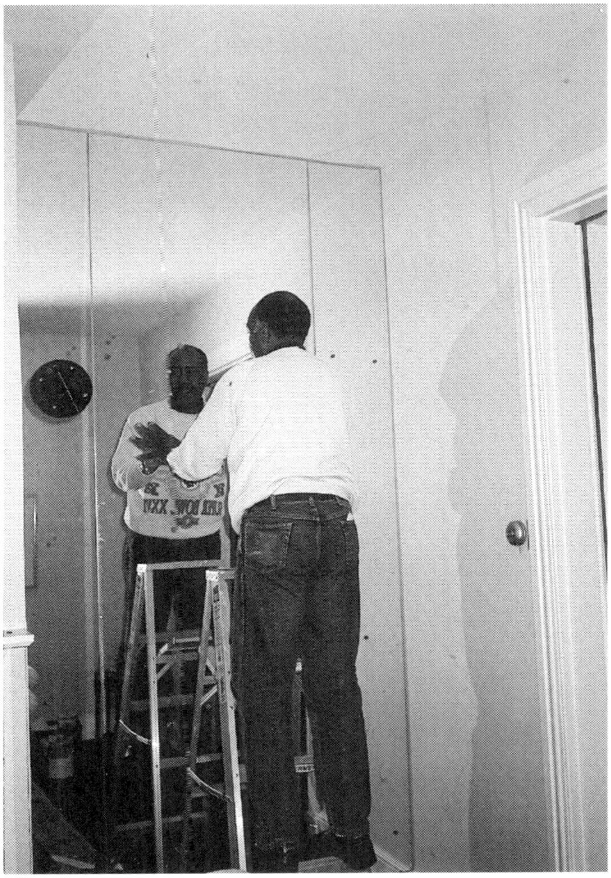

Installation of Mirror in a Bathroom

Even though mirror mastic is strong, most installers recommend resting the bottom edge of the mirror on a lip of tile or a backsplash, with neoprene setting blocks at the bottom of the mirror. Another option is L channel at the bottom of the mirror, once again with setting blocks. If the mirror rests directly on the counter, there is more danger of the splashing of water and entrapment of water; setting blocks are a necessity in this case. While some like the appearance of J mold around the mirror, it can easily trap water. If J mold is used, it should have weep holes installed in it to drain water. The result of the entrapment of water will be "black edge."

Mastic especially formulated for mirrors is a necessity. Certain adhesives, such as silicone, can corrode the backing. Mirror adhesives are available in asphalt-based, rubber-based, or quick-setting formulas.

Asphalt-based mastic is the most commonly used. It remains pliable for three or four days, which is a great advantage if the installer does not put the mirror exactly plumb. It is important that the surface behind the mirror is primed. Untreated plywood or drywall will draw moisture out of the asphalt.

Rubber-based mastic forms a bond quickly, within six hours. Tape or clips keep the mirror in place while the adhesive is curing.

Quick-setting mastic takes only four hours to form a bond. Some mastics are designed for unprimed porous surfaces. Others are designed for nonporous surfaces, such as tile.

Installation of Overmantel Mirror

Boiserie method

Bill Adair of Gold Leaf Studios in Washington, DC, uses the French "boiserie" (meaning woodwork) method of installing overmantel mirrors. He does not like using mastic with mirrors. Initially, a wooden ledge is set on the wall to accept the bottom of the mirror and to support it. Adair then attaches triangular pieces of wood at the upper corners. They are attached to the substrate with screws or nails. On top of that he installs a fascia board, trim to cover the edges, as well as any wood or composition trim or ornaments.

Using the mantel as a support

The simplest way to achieve a built-in effect is to rest the bottom of the mirror directly on the mantel itself, then install a rabbeted frame on the sides.

Supported by trim

Another approach would be to have a bottom piece of rabbeted trim, say two inches above the mantel, screwed into the wall to become a ledge on which to rest the mirror. The mirror is then brought in, and the sides and top of the trim are added.

Metal fasteners

Other methods of attachment are metal clips on the top, bottom, and sides of the mirror. The wood trim applied on top of that should be notched to allow for the thickness of the metal clip. Some use L mold at the bottom of the glass, with wood trim applied on top of that.

Pier Mirrors

Pier mirrors and various mirrors set into panels can be installed in similar fashion to overmantel mirrors. Traditional trim will complete the process. It is always desirable to paint the inside of the rabbeted trim gold or black, so that unfinished wood will not be reflected by the mirror. The thicker the glass, the more will be seen, for the wood will be that much farther away from the reflecting plane.

Mirrored Doors

For those wanting the look of a flush mirror door, it is not recommended that mirror be installed on hollow-core doors, nor is it recommended that mirror be installed on doors solely with mastic. Tape-backed safety mirrors are recommended for installation on doors, with L molding at the bottom of the door to support the weight of the mirrors. The door itself should be removed, lower L molding installed, mastic applied, then mirror installed on top of that and allowed to cure. Mirrors can be installed with rabeted trim on flush doors.

Exterior or interior doors with multiple lights can be utilized with mirror instead of clear glass. One approach might be ⅛" mirror laminated to another sheet of ⅛" mirror, inserted in a door frame designed for ¼" clear glass.

Mirrored Ceiling

It is recommended that mirror approximately 2 feet on a side be used. The outer edges can be supported by clips, J mold or wooden trim. The inner edges must be supported; the usual method is with rosettes, which can support four corners of glass. Mastic can also be used in conjunction with the mirrors, but it is not recommended that it be used alone.

Cleaning of Mirrors

The North American Mirror Manufacturers recommend cleaning mirrors with a solution of 1½ cups of rubbing alcohol per gallon of warm water. They do not recommend using abrasives or harsh alkalis, acids, or ammonia-based cleaners. Additionally, they do not recommend spraying cleaners directly on the mirrors, but, instead, suggest applying the cleaner first to a soft cloth or paper towel.

Bibliography

Adair, William B. *The Frame in America, 1860–1960.* Washington, D.C.: The Federal Reserve Board, exhibition catalogue, 1995.

Adam, Robert. *The Drawings of Robert & James Adam in Sir John Soane's Museum.* Cambridge, U.K.: Somerset House, 1978.

Adams, William Howard. *Jefferson's Monticello.* New York: Abbeville Press, 1983.

Anlen, Leon and Roger Padiou. *Les miroirs de bronze anciens.* Paris: Guy Tredaniel Editiur, 1989.

Baker, Cozy. *Kaleidoscope Renaissance.* Annapolis: Beechcliff Books, 1993.

Baldwin, Billy. *Billy Baldwin Decorates.* New York: Holt, Rinehart and Winston (A House & Garden Book).

Balsdon, J. P. V. D. *Roman Women.* New York: Barnes & Noble Books, 1963.

Beard, Geoffrey. *The National Trust Book of English Furniture.* New York: Viking Penguin Books (in association with the National Trust), 1986.

Beny, Roloff. *Persia, the Bridge of Turquoise.* London: Thames and Hudson, Ltd. 1975.

Blondel, Jacques Francois. *De la distribution des maisons de plaisance.* Vol. 11. Paris: Charles-Antoine Jombert, 1738.

Bourne, Jonathan, ed. *The History of Furniture.* New York: William Morrow, 1976.

Carmody, John and Raymond Sterling. *Underground Space Design.* New York: Van Nostrand Reinhold, 1993.

Child, Graham. *World Mirrors.* London: Sotheby's Publications, 1990.

Chippendale, Thomas. *The Gentleman and Cabinet-maker's Director.* London: Thomas Chippendale, 1754.

Comstock, Helen. *The Looking Glass in America, 1700–1825.* New York: Viking Press, 1968.

Constantine, Ruth. *How to Know French Antiques.* New York: Clarkson Potter, 1961.

De Blancourt, Haudicquer. *The Art of Glass.* London: 1699.

Delaney, Frank. *The Celts.* Boston: Little, Brown and Co., 1986.

Deveche, Andre. *Quatre noms qui ont fait Versailles: Le Brun, Le Notre, Le Vau, Mansart.* Paris: Editions de la Tourelle, 1974.

Diderot, Denis. *A Diderot Encyclopedia of Trades and Industry.* 2 vols., ed. Gillispie, Charles C. New York: Dover Publications, Inc., Pictorial Archive Series, 1987.

Engle, Anita. *Light: Lamps and Windows in Antiquity.* Jerusalem: Phoenix Publications, 1987.

Frame, Donald M. (Trans.). *The Complete Essays of Montaigne.* Stanford: Stanford University Press, 1976.

Gies, Frances and Joseph. *Cathedral, Forge and Waterwheel. Technology and Invention in the Middle Ages.* New York: HarperCollins, 1994.

Goldberg, Benjamin. *The Mirror and Man.* Charlottesville: University Press of Virginia, 1985.

Gombrich, E. H. *Art and Illusion.* Princeton: Princeton University Press, 1972.

Hartlaub, G. F. *Zauber des Spiegels.* Munich: R. Piper & Co., 1951.

Hatfield, Elaine and Susan Sprecher. *Mirror, Mirror: The Importance of Looks in Everyday Life.* Albany: State University of New York Press, 1986.

Hepplewhite, George. *The Cabinet-maker and Upholsterer's Guide.* London: 1794. Reprinted, New York: Dover Publications, 1995.

Heyne, Pamela. *Today's Architectural Mirror.* New York: Van Nostrand Reinhold, 1982.

Hoag, John D. *Western Islamic Architecture.* New York, George Braziller, 1963.

Hollander, Anne. *Seeing Through Clothes.* London: Penguin, 1993.

Hopkins, Albert A. *Magic.* New York: Munn and Co., 1901

Jope, E. M. *Studies in Building History.* Longacre, U.K.: Odhans Press Ltd., 1964.

Jung, Carl G. *Man and His Symbols.* New York: Doubleday and Co., 1964.

Kuo Li Ky Kung Po Wu Yuan. *Masterpieces of Chinese Bronze Mirrors in the National Palace Museum.* Taipei, Taiwan: The National Palace Museum, 1971.

Le Brun, Charles. *Le Brun a Versailles.* 85e exposition du Cabinet des Dessins, Musee du Louvre, 3 October, 1985. Paris: Ministere de la culture, Editions de la Reunion des Musees Nationaux, 1985. (catalogue by Lydia Beauvais and Jean-Francois Mejanes.)

Marot, Daniel. *Uvres contenant plussieurs penseez utile aux architects, peintres, sculpteurs, orfeures & jardiners, & autres.* France: La Haye, P. Hasson, Marchand Libraire, 1700.

Mehrabian, Albert. *Public Places and Private Spaces: The Psychology of Work, Play and Living Environments.* New York: Basic Books, 1976.

Melamed, Elissa. *Mirror, Mirror: The Terror of Not Being Young.* New York: Simon & Schuster, 1983.

Michael, George. *The Overlook Treasury of Federal Antiques.* Woodstock: The Overlook Press, 1986.

Newman, Jay Hartley and Lee Scott Newman. *The Mirror Book.* New York: Crown Publishers, 1978.

Northend, Mary. *Colonial Homes and Their Furnishings.* Boston: Little, Brown and Co., 1912.

Panati, Charles. *Extraordinary Origins of Everyday Things.* New York: Harper & Row, 1987.

Perouse de Montclos, Jean-Marie. *Versailles.* New York: Abbeville Press, 1991.

Polak, Ada. *The Domestic Glass Window.* Reprint of a Glass Circle Lecture, #160. Corning: Rakow Library.

Repton, Humphrey and J. A. Repton. *Fragments on the Theory and Practice of Landscape Gardening.* London: T. Bensley and Son, 1816.

Roche, Serge. *Mirrors.* London: Gerald Duckworth & Co., 1957.

Rossbach, Sarah. *Feng Shui, The Chinese Art of Placement.* New York: Penguin, 1983.

Rossbach, Sarah. *Interior Design with Feng Shui.* New York: E. P. Dutton, 1987.

Rossbach, Sarah and Lin Yun. *Living Color.* New York: Kodansha International, 1994.

Sheraton, Thomas. *The Cabinet-Maker and Upholsterer's Drawing-Book.* New York: Praeger Publishers, 1970.

Sheraton, Thomas. *The Furniture Designs of Thomas Sheraton.* Arranged by J. Munro Bell; with an introduction and critical estimate by Arthur Hayden. London: Gibbens & Co., 1910.

Schiffer, Herbert F. *The Mirror Book: English, American and European.* Exton, Pennsylvania: Schiffer Publishing, 1983.

Van Der Kamp, Gerald, Simone Hoog, and Daniel Meyer. *Versailles.* Paris: Bussiere Arts Graphiques, 1988.

Zerwick, Chloe. *A Short History of Glass.* New York: Harry N. Abrams (in association with The Corning Museum of Glass), 1990.

Zimmer, Gerhard. *Spiegel im Antikenmuseum.* Berlin: Mann, 1987.

Index

O

P

Q

R